CW00815869

REFLECTIONS

Pat Barfoot

With Best
Wishes.

Pat.

Pen Press Publishers Ltd

First published in Great Britain by
Pen Press Publishers Ltd
39-41, North Road
Islington
London N7 9DP

ISBN 1-905203-92-6

Printed and bound in the UK

A catalogue record of this book is available from
the British Library

Cover design by Jacqueline Abromeit

About the Author

Pat Barfoot was born in Seaford, Sussex, in 1930 and was educated at Rye Grammar School, Bishop Otter College, Chichester and Brighton College of Art.

She taught art, crafts, English, drama and P.E. in Kent, Sussex, Kenya, New Zealand and Lincolnshire, retiring in 1985. From 1973 to 1981 she also ran a studio pottery in Lincolnshire.

Pat's interests have included amateur dramatics, writing, photography and sport, especially golf which she still plays. Having edited various school publications over the years and the 1904-2004 Centenary book of her golf club, she felt it was time to publish some of her more personal writing, much of which relates to the time she spent working abroad.

CONTENTS

GITEMU'S DILEMMA

Giant shadows played on the mud walls and grass thatch as Gitemu's large family gathered for the evening meal by the light of the hurricane lamp.

"Ndolo has left home again," Lamu told her husband as she took her place beside him. As head-man he needed to know who was living in the village.

"Munyu does not know why, or where her son has gone, but she is troubled by his going yet again."

Gitemu relied on the women's well-side gossip to keep himself informed, though he did not believe everything his wife told him. What man would?

"Munyu complains that he came home briefly only because he needed her healing powers on a wound he carried," Lamu continued in her gentle voice.

Gitemu's lined face showed no sign of having heard his wife's report, but he was considering her words and storing the information away in his unfailing memory. As he ate, his mind was drawing together all the previous reports of Ndolo's erratic behaviour, searching for a pattern. He had heard that enmity existed between Ndolo and his half-brother, Moika, and that for many moons past Ndolo had spent long periods away from the village, returning only briefly to his father's house, then leaving it as suddenly. This was not the way of his people. The whole village knew whenever one of their number left to collect a new bride or attend the funeral of a kinsman or, rarely, to find work in the township. No one's movements or purpose were secret, no one but Ndolo, that is.

Gitemu was glad that his sons had not left the village. He knew it would be different with the following generation. He sought out his eldest grandson, Joseph, soon to start at the High School in Machakos, and thought he saw a memory of himself at the same age, but his grandson could read anything and knew much English. Perhaps he would be a teacher one day, or even sit in the government in Nairobi.

Though Gitemu could not read he was Mzee, the wise village elder who cared deeply for his people. His wisdom and dignity commanded the respect of the whole village, and beyond.

Seeing Moika the following day, Gitemu asked where his brother had gone. Moika dropped his gaze, shrugged and disrespectfully turned away. "Nairobi perhaps," he answered roughly. "I cannot tell what my half-brother will do."

Though Gitemu could not read books he could read people and he was disturbed by Moika's evasive answer. The young man could not meet his eyes when he spoke and he was certain he was lying. He was saddened too, by his lack of respect. The day following that meeting Munyu came to Gitemu's hut and asked to see the head-man. It was not usual for a woman to seek such a meeting and Gitemu asked why her husband, Wambua, had not come himself.

"He will not come," said the woman, her face drawn and closed, "and he does not know that I have come, but I must speak with you."

"It is not our custom," replied Gitemu gently, "but if you are troubled I will hear you."

"My son Ndolo," Munyu began, then stopped.

"Yes, what of your son? I hear he has gone away again," the old man prompted.

"I thought so," Munyu continued, becoming agitated. "I thought so but I know now that this is not so. I heard Moika talking with his father late last night. He has killed my son, his half-brother."

"Killed Ndolo?" Gitemu queried, in stunned disbelief.

"That is what Moika himself said, yet Wambua says he will protect him! One son kills another and their father shows no anger. I had to come. My only son is dead and his killer goes unpunished."

The head-man was silent. What must he do? He alone was responsible for the law and customs. His voice troubled, he questioned Munyu further. "Wife of Wambua, these are serious words you speak; are you certain of what you say?"

"I am certain. It was dark and they could not see me, but I heard Moika say that they had fought and that Ndolo was dead by his hand. Moika himself carries a fresh wound on his chest."

"What more did you hear? Think carefully."

"I heard Wambua say that the family would be shamed and Moika must tell no one, not even his mother. I thought I should be discovered then, so I moved into the hut. Wambua has said nothing of all this to me."

"You do right to tell me. Tell no one of these matters. Go now."

All that night Gitemu pondered what he must do. He knew that he should report this business to the police post at Makuyuni, yet he was troubled. All the village people trusted him and Wambua was his friend; but unless his friend was open with him, what was such a friendship worth?

In the morning he sent a son to find Wambua and to ask him, with respect, to come to see him. Wambua came, but he did not seem at ease and Gitemu called for a pot of maize beer to lessen the tension of a difficult meeting. For a while they drank and exchanged trivialities until, finally, Gitemu introduced the purpose of their meeting.

"Wambua, you and I are friends of many years."

"That is true, Gitemu. We have been friends since you were my sponsor at my circumcision, because I had no father living."

"I do not say this easily then, but I must ask you, as head-man, why you hold back from me and are not open in your speaking?"

Wambua's eyes widened at this but he quickly regained his control, for he could not see how Gitemu could know what he chose to hide from him.

"I am always open with you, Mzee," he replied formally.

Gitemu was saddened by Wambua's deceit. "You reminded me just now, Wambua, that I took the place of your father at your circumcision. As your sponsor as well as your head-man, I ask you to be honest with me. I hear disturbing stories about your two sons, Ndolo and Moika." Gitemu paused, giving Wambua a chance to speak.

He saw that Wambua was sweating profusely and noted the fear shadowing his eyes, saw too that Wambua was bewildered, at a loss. But, taking control once more, to Gitemu he said: "Ndolo has gone away: Moika stays at home. What more can I say?"

"You could be honest with me and tell me that Ndolo is dead, killed by his brother, Moika," Gitemu replied quietly.

Wambua trembled and sweated more freely, fear and superstition surfacing.

"How can you know these things?" he cried, his eyes wide and staring.

"I am Mzee. I know many things," Gitemu replied with great dignity. Then: "You know that I must report this," he added, his voice flat and resigned.

"No, you cannot. One son is dead. If you report Moika they will take him from me and I shall have no son. I beg you, do not report this."

"Even for you, Wambua, you who are like another son to me, I cannot hide this crime. Tell me all you know. Perhaps Moika had just cause?"

But Wambua was beyond reasoning, in the grip of fear. "No Gitemu, no! I have always respected you and obeyed you as my elder, but if you do this thing you will die! The old wives of Kuenga will help me," he threatened and fled from the hut.

The threat was not an idle one, Gitemu knew. He was a Christian but his primitive roots ran deep. He knew the reputation held by the old wives, a reputation for witchcraft. He also knew strong men who had succumbed to their potent spells. He spent another sleepless night struggling with his conscience and his fears. He had a duty, but he was afraid. He could not dispel his fear of witchcraft, even by prayer.

He knew that Wambua could not have slept that night either, for he had seen him set off across the hills to Kuenga. For some hard-earned shillings and the young goat he was carrying, Gitemu knew he would have bought the evil services of the old wives — and the promise of his death should he report Moika. Gitemu knew the risk was real.

Early morning mist enveloped the village. Slowly it began to lift but the profound silence persisted. Ribbons of vapour drifted about the walls of the huts, barely stirring in the still air. Above the mist the grass-thatched roofs appeared to float, unsupported. Spiders' webs, heavy with moisture, clung to the thorn brush enclosing the boma penning the animals.

No bird welcomed the day, no goat bleated and the usually vociferous dogs were silent, their hair standing in ridges on their backs as they cowered, sensing the evil abroad on the clammy air. A bedraggled dead chicken hung from the lintel of Gitemu's doorway, which Wambua watched with steady, unswerving menace. Evil attended his presence in the mist.

As he stepped from his hut, Gitemu's face was brushed by the wet feathers of the hanging chicken. His heart froze and cold sweat beaded his forehead. Peering into the mist he barely distinguished the malevolent form of Wambua, though he felt his presence only too keenly. But Gitemu had come through the struggles of the night and knew that he had no choice in the matter. He tore the chicken from the wall and flung it at Wambua's feet.

"You must know what I have to do, Wambua. It saddens me but I have no choice. Your threats have no strength against a Christian." And he turned away, full of grief for a lost friendship, and not totally convinced by his brave show of faith.

By 7 o'clock he was on his way to Makuyuni to report to the police. With heavy heart he had made his farewells to Lamu and his family for he knew that he might not return. His sons, knowing only that he had to visit Makuyuni and not the reason, would willingly have gone in his stead but he had refused. This journey was one only he could undertake. The responsibility was his alone; the danger must be his also.

It was a long and perilous trek and Gitemu was an old man. He had slept little for two nights past and fear sapped his strength. One cannot overcome the superstitions of generations with a few prayers.

As the sun burned away the mist of the morning, the temperature rose sharply and Gitemu suffered the first symptoms of distress. He felt that every step he took was being watched by evil eyes. He sensed the malevolent gaze of supernatural forces following him from behind each clump of spiky sisal, each rocky outcrop. He looked neither right nor left but kept his eyes upon the stony path he followed.

Four miles then five and the sun beat upon the old man. Six miles, and the tightness in his chest made his breathing shallow and difficult. Seven miles and his breathing became rasping and painful, his distress obvious.

He rested in the shade afforded by a solitary thorn tree. He drank a little water from his goatskin bag and ate a mouthful of posho porridge which Lamu had wrapped in a piece of cloth. He slept briefly yet heavily and woke with guilt, for he had not intended to sleep.

He had to reach Makuyuni before his strength and purpose were spent. He rose and, leaning on his staff, continued his painful progress towards his goal. He was not aware of having dreamt but he sensed an added burden of evil upon his shoulders.

In the extreme heat of noon his chest pains multiplied and his breathing grew even more laboured. The red murram dust of the path invaded his scorched lungs and threatened to choke the life from him. "He's winning," Gitemu thought in anguish. "Wambua is winning and I shall die before I reach Makuyuni."

He struggled on over stony ground and across dried river beds where the sun's heat was cruelly thrown back at him from the smooth rock slabs, increasing his distress. He began to mouth a prayer and a crumb of comfort came to him. "If you do this thing you will die." Those were the words Wambua had used. So, threat of death would come only after he had made his report; he would have an opportunity to make it.

Early in the afternoon, with the sun at its fiercest, he laboured up the rise towards his destination. A band of iron bit deeply into his heart and he gasped for air. As he arrived at the police post he collapsed at the feet of an askari standing guard beside the steps. The askari called to another and together they carried Gitemu, more dead than alive, into the building and laid him upon a bench.

In his semi-conscious state his purpose was not forgotten, for he mumbled and muttered continuously: "Ndolo — have to report — must do it — my duty — Ndolo Wambua — —".

An officer behind the desk looked up, his attention drawn by the old man's mutterings. He walked over to where Gitemu lay prostrate upon the bench.

"Mzee, can you hear me?" he asked. "What is it you are trying to say? Who is this Ndolo Wambua? Who is he? What has he done?"

Increased consciousness returned to Gitemu in response to a wet cloth being placed on his forehead and he sipped the water held to his lips. The mist inside his head was clearing but his straining heart and lungs still threatened to burst. He could hear, from beyond the pain, the officer talking to a subordinate.

"Fetch me the Game Department's recent report on the ivory poaching gang. It may be a coincidence but this name, Ndolo, sounds familiar. Here, let me see it: ' — *ruthless gang of ivory poachers — Amboseli Reserve — two killed by askaris eighteen days ago — several wounded and captured'*. Yes, here it is: *'One, Ndolo Wambua from Ngoa district, escaped capture but was thought to be wounded'.* Could this be the same man?"

Gitemu made a supreme effort to muster his concentration. "So," he thought, "this must be the same Ndolo whose murder I've come to report. No wonder the family would be shamed! Ndolo was a man who killed for money and not to stem his hunger, a thief with no respect for the mighty elephant. So, Moika had just cause to punish his half-brother. He shall not pay for that." He summoned all his strength and raised himself on one elbow. "I've come from Ngoa district," he said hoarsely. "I've come to report — ", but his voice faded and he lay back exhausted.

The officer bent over him. "What is that, Mzee? Ngoa district you say?"

"Yes, I have come to report — ", but again his voice trailed off.

"To report what, Mzee?"

"To report — to report an accident," Gitemu finally managed. "Ndolo Wambua from my village was killed by — by falling rocks two days ago. His brother saw it happen."

He lay back, relaxed, breathing more deeply, his heart returning to its normal steady beat, his conscience untroubled, his doubts resolved.

DROUGHT — EAST AFRICA

Rains failed, no rains. Dry earth on the dusty plains.

The cows plod on, scrawny beasts, from dried-up runnel to bare-grazed earth.

The sun stares down, dispelling hope, as dust devils spiral high above.

One more step, the cow bells jangle, one more step, no lowing's heard.

One more step, parched throats are silent. One last step — return to dust.

A carcass lies on the cruel earth, skin drawn close on brittle frame:

Food for flies and worms and vultures, ashes to ashes and dust to dust.

And still the sun burns through the haze, and still the rain withholds its balm,

And dust devils rise and hang in the air — over the barren land.

The smell of death is everywhere, the smell of death amid the dust.

Clouds in the sky, a sunless glare hangs weightily over the plain.

The ranging hills begin to moan, thunder rumbles in the air,

Oppressive heat — stillness complete, till with a roar the sky is rent.

Raindrops strike the dust and sink; the thirsty earth drinks in.

A new smell permeates the air: raindrops falling on the dust.

The river once more starts to flow; water holes refill again;

Grass long thought dead shoots forth a brave green finger to the sky;

The dead earth struggles back to life; the cycle is complete.

The lowing herd, with jangling bells, with lighter steps moves on.

The Masai boy looks on and laughs, and life is good again.

Kenya, August 1961.

DAY OF JUDGEMENT

Dennis Yeats stormed out of the courtroom, his mean face puce with rage and frustration. In the corridor he confronted his uncle Joe who, naturally enough, was feeling relieved by the judgement.

"O.K. so you've won the first battle, Joe, but I'm not ready to concede; I shall appeal against this decision," Dennis said with considerable malice. "Tenant's rights! What about owner's rights?"

"Dennis lad, I didn't want to bring the law into it but you left me no choice." Joe's tone was conciliatory. "The smallholding's my livelihood as well as my home. If you're honest you'll admit that your dad meant me to continue living there for life. After that you can build whatever you like on it, a skyscraper as far as I'm concerned. All I shall need then is a six foot plot."

Dennis leaned over his uncle in a threatening manner. "Sooner the better in my opinion," he declared venomously. "Why you can't move into a retirement flat I don't know. Save us all a lot of trouble. You've held up my plans long enough. It's two years since I first got planning permission. Do you know what that's worth?" he asked.

Joe nodded. "A great deal, I'm sure, but you've other irons in the fire. You don't really need my three acres yet awhile. Besides, I couldn't face being shut up in a flat."

Dennis was not mollified. "Well, I haven't finished, not by a long chalk. I intend to develop that site. Tenancy protection be damned; I was a fool not to have contested that bit of Dad's will at the time. You don't even make full use of it these days. Wasted land!" he accused, turning on his heel and striding from the building. He drove off in his Mercedes, leaving Joe to travel the same route by bus. Joe shook his old head sadly and tears stung his tired eyes. He had not enjoyed taking his nephew to court to establish his rights but what option had he? He had enjoyed his life on the smallholding for more than 50 years, and anyway, how else could he scrape a living if he had to move off the property?

Dennis's court appeal failed. He was furious, but there was no more to be done, or was there? He was not a good loser; on the contrary, he was one of life's winners, a self-made millionaire and proud of it.

"I will not be thwarted," he threatened his uncle after the abortive appeal hearing. He no longer had faith in the law which had ruled against him.

Despite his victory, Joe went home a much saddened man. Another couple of years and Dennis could have the lot, he thought, his bungalow and the land, the whole shooting match. He was sure he would not have any use for it by then. He looked much older than his seventy years. He suddenly looked a frail old man.

Joe woke up the next morning feeling slightly uneasy. He could not say why but something felt wrong. He peered into the bathroom mirror, rubbing his balding head with a gnarled hand. A dose of salts was all he needed, he decided, reaching for the jar in the medicine cabinet. "Expect I'm just a bit liverish this morning," he told his reflection. He dressed in his dungarees, went through to the kitchen and started to fill the kettle.

"My God!" he exclaimed, as he saw the devastation wreaked upon his land. Staring through the window, he whispered in disbelief: "It looks like a battlefield".

Indeed it did. Chaos lay everywhere Joe looked, as he surveyed the scene from the back door. His shoulders slumped and his lined face wore a pained expression. Closer inspection revealed that the soft fruit bushes, which Joe had tended so lovingly over the years, had been uprooted and spattered with diesel. Every cabbage had been slashed to pieces, likewise the cauliflowers. Shredded leeks and carrots, and even chopped up hosepipe had been ground into the earth.

Joe knew that Dennis would not have soiled his well manicured hands to create this mess but he had no doubt that he had paid others to do his dirty work for him. Along with the outrage, Joe felt sickened with shame that his own nephew could stoop so low.

He spent a week salvaging what could be salvaged and clearing the debris. It was hard work for the old man. Thankfully, the two large greenhouses and the chickens were untouched and Joe kept going on the income from these. If Dennis thought he could be driven out of his home so easily, he was heading for disillusion.

A couple of weeks later, however, Joe's place was devastated by a second night of wanton destruction.

His chickens were hanging from the rafters of the henhouse, their necks wrung, Dennis's henchmen had made no attempt to cast the blame on a fox! Luckily, Joe was able to sell the poultry to a local butcher. He knew he should have reported the incidents but he could not bring himself to air the family's dirty washing in public.

A week or two later Dennis stepped from his front door just as the post van arrived at the gates. "I'll take the mail," he said, and he stuffed several envelopes into his pocket as the postman drove off.

"Now don't you worry, Bill," he told his JCB driver, who had parked a little beyond the gates. "The responsibility's all mine, and after all, it's my own property. What can the law do except fine me a packet? It will be worth it to finally shift the old fool." They mounted the JCB and drove down the lane to Joe's smallholding.

"What if the old man's there?" Bill asked his employer nervously.

"He's not," Dennis assured him. "That's why I rang you. I saw him get on the town bus. The first bus back is not for three hours. By that time we shall be past the point of no return. Stop worrying."

"You're the boss, but I don't feel happy about it. Anyway, it's a waste, and I hate waste," Bill complained.

"So you're right, it is a waste, but it's the only way to shift him. It will pay me in the long run, you too — £500 for a day's work!" Dennis was matey suddenly, clapping Bill on the shoulder, persuading him he was a good bloke.

As expected, the smallholding was deserted when they arrived. "First job is to move all Joe's belongings onto that hard-standing there. I can't leave the old devil nothing to set up home with somewhere else," Dennis admitted.

It took them over an hour to move everything out, longer than Dennis had expected. Then, a note of triumph in his voice, Dennis instructed the driver: "Right, now get on with it, Bill".

The JCB roared into life and Bill drove at one corner of the bungalow. There was a loud crunch as the monster battered into the wall, loosening a dozen or so bricks. Each subsequent charge did a little more damage, until the corner of the roof sagged and crashed to the ground. It proved a much tougher job than Dennis had anticipated, for the bungalow was very well built and in good repair, but by mid morning it was a sorry sight, no longer habitable.

"Two walls down and two to go, Bill!" Dennis shouted above the thunder of the machine: "Take a break!" He took a hip flask from his pocket.

At that moment a pantechnicon drove through the gate. Joe jumped out looking more spritely than for some time past and when he saw Dennis he grinned broadly.

"Well, Dennis lad," the old man greeted him cheerfully. "I see you aren't wasting any time. Never put off till tomorrow, eh?" Dennis was completely bewildered by his uncle's unexpected attitude, and was rendered speechless. "I didn't post the letter till yesterday," Joe continued. "All's well that ends well, as your dad used to say. No hard feelings, eh?"

Still dumbstruck, Dennis took Joe's proffered hand and shook it.

"Letter?" he queried faintly, fumbling in his jacket pocket.

"Ay, the one telling you I'd come up on the lottery, a pretty useful sum. I've bought a small bungalow on the outskirts of town, nice little bit of garden. It's time I retired, really. Now I can afford to." Joe was beaming, as happy as a pig in muck.

Dennis, on the other hand, gave the appearance of being turned to stone, a gaping gargoyle.

"Come on then, better get the van loaded, eh?" Joe addressed the van driver and his mate. "Thanks for stacking all my things here, very considerate." Then, as he walked towards his belongings, he threw his parting shot at his nephew. "I can't see the need to demolish the bungalow. Must be worth about £150,000 or more - leastways, it was. Still, that's not my loss, is it Dennis lad?"

And Dennis was left to contemplate his costly day of judgement.

THE WASTELANDS

The land is dry.
The grass is brittle
And crunches underfoot.
Barren is the land.

The sun beats down,
Unmerciful its glare,
Parching the earth.
A thirsty land.

The hot wind blows.
The withering wind
Lays waste the plain.
A windswept land.

My heart is bare.
My soul is void and numb.
I crave the life I know.
A distant land.

The land is dry.
My soul is thirsting too.
Rains, come down for the soil.
Come, comfort of the soul.

Machakos 1959

A BORROWED ROOF

"£13,852!" Vicky almost screamed it in disbelief, running a frantic hand through her coppery hair. "How could Dad have owed so much, and to a bookmaker of all people!"

She had heard that disasters preferred to travel in convoy but this was ridiculous. Bad news was a daily occurrence since her bereavement two weeks earlier. Her father's cottage, her cottage now, needed re-tiling urgently, and that was just for starters. The bank manager had declared her inherited bonds virtually worthless and Aggy had failed her MOT by some distance.

"£13,852?" she repeated, fire-flecked hazel eyes threatening to incinerate the offending letter. "They'll be lucky to get the 52 just at present!" Vicky wondered how her father had managed to place the bets while he was housebound. She concluded that he must have been more adept at using his mobile than he'd let on. And why had the debt been allowed to grow to such a figure?

Many young women in the position she now found herself in would have wilted or waited for the bailiffs to move in, not Vicky. Luckily she was a realist, eminently practical and level headed. She knew exactly what had to be done.

She had been an efficient secretary in a publishing house but she felt that her skills must have rusted while she had nursed her father through his long illness. Anyway, live-in secretaries were a rare breed she realised, and what she needed above all, quite literally, was a roof over her head.

Somewhat reluctantly she parted with Aggy, selling the car for a pathetic £350. Of the furniture, she stored the best and sold the rest. She advertised the cottage as "ripe for modernisation" and herself as "a resident housekeeper, girl Friday, companion; anything legal considered, references exchanged".

* * * *

The agent, a dapper, busy little man, met Vicky from the train and drove her out to Cedar House. She thought how fresh and inviting the countryside looked, newly washed on that sparkling afternoon in late April.

The imposing pillars at the entrance gave Vicky her first impression, the avenue of ancient cedars confirmed it and the first sight of the house itself confounded expectation. "This isn't a house," she thought, "it's a country estate! How could the owners bear to leave all this to work in the Gulf ?"

They were met by George who, cap in hand, fulfilled all Vicky's ideas of the old family retainer. He introduced her three charges, an odd assortment: a handsome Dalmation, a perky Highland Terrier and a Siamese cat of superior breeding and eccentric character.

After a brief tour of the house and a more thorough explanation of the high-tech security system, the agent handed over the keys, including a set for a roomy estate car.

"As explained in the contract, all accounts for the house, the garden and the car are my responsibility. Just forward them to my office. George's wife will spend two hours three times a week on general cleaning in the house. They are both paid by me and your salary will be paid into your account on the first of each month. If you encounter any problems at all Miss Fielding, give me a ring. Office and home numbers are both on my card. Good day to you."

Vicky whistled happily as she took her luggage to a comfortable south-facing bedroom. She postponed her unpacking; two cases and a word processor would not take long anyway. She went to the large, well equipped kitchen, followed closely by Pierot, Angus and Taipo.

The animals sat in a row, an incongruous trio, while Vicky made a pot of tea and found a tin of biscuits. She chose a homely kitchen pot of brown earthenware in preference to the drawing-room silver. She felt at home 'below stairs' and the kitchen was a very welcoming place. She drank several cups of tea while the animals watched and waited, showing impeccable manners.

"Come on then," Vicky said to her charges. "Show me the gardens before dark."

Vicky led the way into the vast grounds, accompanied by the three musketeers, and explored for over half an hour. George was still working in the large greenhouse.

"There's plenty of veg, Miss," he offered. "You just

'as to tell me what you want. Some things ent ready yet, a course, but most spring veg and some salad stuff's about."

Vicky thanked him and took a trug basket full of fresh vegetables away with her. "I can see I'm going to enjoy a healthy diet, George. These look a great deal more inviting than some of the tired ones I've seen in the shops."

The sun was behind the cedars by the time Vicky called the pets together to return indoors. "I'm so glad you answer to your names so readily. I shan't be afraid to take you beyond the walls," she said, with much relief.

That evening she began keeping a diary of her new lifestyle. "Who knows, maybe I'll develop a talent for writing. Time on my hands will give me a chance to find out," she considered, as she went to bed, convinced that she would thoroughly enjoy her unusual job in such very pleasant surroundings. It would be akin to a holiday.

The following day she ventured further afield with the animals. Ashdown Forest, she soon discovered, was as much heathland as forest but a great place for walks and the trio obviously enjoyed their outing. "I'll certainly get fit keeping up with you," Vicky told the pets, though she was already fitter than most 30 year olds who play no active part in sport.

No sooner had she driven the estate out of the garage the following Sunday than the trio had lined up, ready to jump aboard. "You really are an odd bunch! If I'm going to break into print I could do worse than start with you three. I must buy a camera to capture your eccentricities," she decided.

First to the newsagents for the Sunday papers, then to a more distant area of the forest where she parked off the road. For an hour or more the animals romped while Vicky read the papers. At noon, as she was about to load the pets, she noticed that the rear off-side tyre was almost flat.

"Oh heavens!" she cried, realising that she had not even checked the spare. "Good old George," she said as she discovered the spare fully inflated. The jack was another matter. It was a type quite foreign to Vicky and she was still studying it and the anchorage points when a smart sports car drew into the clearing.

The driver, casually dressed in jeans and an open necked shirt, was festooned with photographic paraphernalia. He let out two Red Setters and walked over to Vicky. "Problems?" he asked with a friendly smile.

"Oh, hello. Yes, I can change a wheel but I can't figure out how this jack operates," Vicky replied, unused to admitting a need for help, even from blond gods with laughing brown eyes and healthy tans.

"May I?" the young man took the device from Vicky. "Ah, I think I can see how it works. Let's put it to the test." Which he did with complete success, while Vicky watched and thought what a handsome young knight he was. She thanked him and returned his cameras after he had stowed the wheel in the back of the estate.

"Hello, I recognise these three characters," he said as the trio broke from the undergrowth. "You must be from Cedar House which makes us neighbours. I've seen these animals in the garden.

"Tom Gregg, The Grange," he said, offering a slightly grubby hand.

"Vicky Fielding. I'm very glad you happened along. I could've been stuck here a while trying to fathom that fearsome jack. As long as we're neighbours you must call in for a thankyou drink sometime."

"Thanks, the sooner the better, if you're serious," Tom replied, keen to meet Vicky again and maybe establish a friendship.

Vicky laughed at his easy manner: "O.K. six o'clock this evening and I'll rustle up some supper as well, if you're free."

"As the birds! Now I mustn't lose Bill and Ben. Till six o'clock," he said, as he went off in search of his dogs. "I look forward to it."

Vicky felt rather pleased with herself as she drove home.

At precisely six Vicky led Tom into a comfortable sitting room overlooking a formal garden, a room which trapped the evening sun.

"I trust you didn't lose Bill and Ben today while doing your Samaritan act. Drink?" she offered.

"G and T please. No,no. I use a special high-pitched whistle and they come post-haste. By the way, Bill and Ben are my pet names. They have quite unmanageable kennel club names but I prefer simplicity. What's the name of your handsome Dalmation?"

"Pierot. Angus is the terrier, Taipo the cat with personality plus. She's convinced she's a dog!" she replied, handing Tom his drink.

"Thanks Vicky. This really is a splendid outlook, most photogenic."

"I take it you're an expert in that field. You were certainly carrying a lot of equipment this morning."

"Yes, I really enjoy it. I have done ever since I was given my first camera when I was about ten," Tom replied with obvious enthusiasm.

"Good, so you'll be able to advise me. I want a cheap camera myself, just for taking snaps, nothing elaborate. What do you suggest?"

Tom thought it strange that Vicky should want a cheap camera, there being such evidence of money all around, but "That's easy," he said. "You can try my 35mm automatic for a bit, see how you like it."

Vicky was embarrassed by Tom's generosity but accepted his offer gratefully.

"I'll bring it over tomorrow," he offered, pleased to have an excuse to call again.

He was as good as his word and he explained how to get the best results. They saw a good deal of each other during the next few weeks and met almost daily on the heath where, luckily, the animals made friends as easily as Vicky and Tom.

Vicky wondered how a young man came by so much leisure time, but decided he must be one of the privileged few who have no need to earn a crust. "Anyway, I certainly can't ask him," Vicky thought. "He would think I was after his money!"

* * * *

Vicky was not unduly surprised, while walking on the heath one morning, when Tom announced: "I've booked a candle-lit table for two at the Cameo for eight o'clock this evening. You will come, won't you? I know I should've asked you first but, well, it's a minor celebration and I suppose I was a bit impetuous."

Vicky thought how disarmingly boyish he looked as a broad smile lit up his face. "Not your birthday, is it?" she asked.

"Nothing so mundane. I've had a bit of good fortune, that's all."

"I'd love to come. Shall I learn the reason for the celebration?"

"In due course maybe," he replied enigmatically. "Half seven, I'll call round for you. Come this way now," he added, taking her hand. "I discovered a really spectacular view yesterday."

Vicky would have liked to ask what sort of luck he'd had but was afraid of prying. "A killing on the exchange, no doubt," she thought.

Accompanied by their assorted animals, Vicky and Tom set off to find the magnificent view from Camp Hill. Slightly breathless, they arrived at the top in glorious sunshine and sat down to rest and enjoy the Sussex countryside in companionable silence. Vicky realised then how much she had been missing congenial company over the previous two years. She felt deprived, and thanked the gods of fortune for bringing Tom into her life.

At full stretch on the grass Tom had to reach up to loosen the ribbon gathering Vicky's coppery hair in a pony tail. She turned, smiling, as she felt his hand pulling the ribbon. He drew her down beside him, kissing her tenderly. She was quick to respond, aware just how starved of affection she was. Their relationship might have blossomed then and there had not the dogs barked in chorus, announcing the untimely arrival of a party of ramblers.

They called the dogs to them as the walkers appeared startled, and the mood was broken. Tom chewed on a grass stalk, his hand resting lightly on Vicky's shoulder. Finding the ribbon, she retied her hair.

"A fine view," one of the ramblers remarked, somewhat awkwardly.

"Right," Tom replied. "Must be able to see for forty miles that way."

The walkers shed their knapsacks, unpacking picnics, cameras, maps and sketch-pads. They obviously intended to stay some while. As Tom and Vicky preferred to be alone just then, they called the animals and left the summit, making their way down, hand in hand.

Having reached the cars, Tom kissed Vicky lightly.

"Seven-thirty," he said.

"I'll be ready, best party frock!" she replied.

That evening they made a very handsome couple and Vicky felt she was being watched and possibly envied, escorted by Tom in this smart little restaurant.

"They're wondering why I'm being wined and dined by the master of The Grange, instead of their high-society daughters," Vicky mused. But she was in no way intimidated; on the contrary their relationship deepened that evening. They each felt more than a passing attraction, yet both were conscious of an unidentified barrier.

"Thank you for making this evening very special, Vicky," Tom said as they arrived back at Cedar House. "I felt so proud to be with the most beautiful woman in the restaurant; everyone's eyes were on you, including mine, needless to say."

Tom kissed her gently and she was almost tempted to invite him in, but she felt that he would have to make the first move. Would he ever do so?

* * * *

The second Sunday in June was a glorious day so Vicky carried her breakfast tray and newspaper out onto the terrace. "I'm growing far too accustomed to this lifestyle," she informed the pets, always good listeners. "Shall I ever be able to work for a living again, in the real world?"

As usual the trio had padded after her and settled comfortably, waiting for crumbs and kind words. Having enjoyed her first cup of coffee she poured a second and opened the colour supplement.

"What the devil?" she almost dropped the cup suddenly, then gave her full attention to the familiar landscape where she and the trio, in the middle distance it's true, sported themselves on the heath.

"Whoever . . ?" but of course she knew the answer even before she could complete the question. She slapped the magazine onto the table, spilling some coffee. She was not best pleased. The caption read 'Ashdown Forest in May', with no reference to her presence. There were three other, smaller photos, all familiar views. The name on the credits confirmed her suspicions.

"What a cheek!" she exclaimed, still staring at the double page spread when Tom arrived, smiling as ever.

"Hi! Lovely day again, so how do we plan to spend it?" he asked, leaning nonchalantly against the balustrade.

"Good morning. You've seen this I presume?" Vicky's tone was icy.

Tom looked over her shoulder. "Just now. Good photos, don't you think?" he said proudly, so pleased with himself that he failed to notice her brittle tone.

He sat down, smiling expansively, and continued to admire the photos.

"I can't argue with that. So you'll have received a fat fee." She snatched the magazine away from his admiring gaze.

"Not bad. £1,500. For the set, of course. My best fee to date. That's why we were celebrating at The Cameo."

"And was my dinner my fee?" An icy edge to Vicky's voice could no longer go unnoticed.

Tom laughed and then, with embarrassment, he realised that Vicky was serious. "I... I'm sorry. I thought you'd be pleased," he stammered, puzzled by Vicky's reaction.

"You didn't think to ask my permission? I simply don't like being taken for granted," she protested.

"I didn't ask your permission because you aren't the subject of the composition. You and the animals are ... incidental."

"But not accidental. You knew the composition needed human interest and I supplied it, unwittingly. Now I want my fee." Vicky was sorry she had started this but seemed unable to stop herself; someone else had taken over.

"Vicky, I'm sorry, really sorry. I wasn't taking you for granted, for heaven's sake; I just wanted to surprise you. I do think you're being unreasonable about a rather trivial matter." Tom looked completely bewildered by Vicky's uncharacteristic attitude.

"Trivial?" She picked on the word and again felt aggrieved. "To you £1500 might be a trivial sum. In that case it won't hurt you to give £150 appearance money, to charity of course.

"You're not serious? Ten percent of my earnings

30

for a middle distance appearance causing you absolutely no inconvenience! A totally painless contribution to a . . a . . an artistic work, and you expect me to cough up £150?"

"Come now, you can well afford it and maybe it'll teach you not to play Lord of the Manor," Vicky goaded him.

"Afford it?" Tom spluttered. "This is my first important acceptance; could help my career prospects, it's true, but I've been working for peanuts for ages, while trying to make the glossies."

"But you don't exactly suffer for your art, do you? No starving in a garret for you." Vicky knew she was being unreasonable but was still unable to stop.

Tom failed to read the implication. "My job enables me to live in a splendid house, granted, but you're a fine one to talk of garrets. As owner of a place like Cedar House I doubt if you have the slightest idea how the other half lives." Tom felt unjustly accused and was beginning to lose his temper at last.

"Owner of? You think all this is mine?" Vicky sounded incredulous.

"Yours, your family's, what's the difference?"

Vicky had a fleeting vision of her father's cottage, with its sagging roof and flaking paint. She started to laugh.

Tom was naturally disconcerted. "What's so funny? If my family owned such a place I most certainly wouldn't find it laughable. I'd be . . ."

"IF they owned?" Vicky interrupted, her woman's instinct starting to work overtime. "But The Grange, what about that?" she added, a small seed of doubt in her voice.

"You think ... good grief," Tom cried. "You think The Grange is mine?"

They stared at each other with puzzled expressions. The penny dropped and Vicky said, "Are you saying The Grange isn't yours?"

"Oh come on now, you must've known I was just caretaking. As a close neighbour you must've known," Tom replied.

"But don't you see, Tom? I'm not a neighbour, close or otherwise. We're neither of us what we seem!" Vicky felt relieved, realising their equal status.

"You mean Cedar House isn't yours either?"

"You're joking! I'm house-sitting, and as a neighbour you'd know it."

"IF I were a neighbour! We're both frauds! What a relief!" He started to laugh and Vicky joined in and they both spoke at once and the pets made a racket so that the Sunday morning calm erupted into a fair imitation of bedlam for several minutes.

"It's picnic weather," Tom announced finally, during a lull in the infectious laughter which surfaced as soon as he and Vicky made eye contact. "I can supply a good bottle of wine, plenty of fruit and probably a crisp or two. How about it?"

"I can find a quiche and there's an assortment of salad in the fridge. Where shall we go?" Vicky asked, her good humour restored.

"Leave that to me, a mystery tour. Shall we go in your car, or the Cedar House car anyway, more room for all the animals. I'll be back pronto with my offerings and Bill and Ben. See you in a few minutes, you imposter!"

* * * *

Sunning themselves beside a gentle stream, replete with good food, wine and bonhomie, their relationship matured and they talked more frankly. They were equals now, almost partners in crime.

"You know, from the first I wondered about you," Vicky admitted. "I couldn't understand how you could afford to squander your time so lazily."

"Mm. Well, I just thought you were filthy rich and idle, probably over-indulged, spoilt rotten. Did wonder why you wanted a cheap camera, though. I concluded you were also mean with your money."

"Beast! If only you knew. What little I have is tied up in a cottage in need of a major face-lift. Well, rather more than that, to be honest." She told Tom about her inheritance, warts an'all, and her need for the job at Cedar House. "The cottage is still on the market. A few people have viewed it but the agent says they lose interest when they see just how much work is needed."

"Does it have character, this cottage?"

"Oh yes, bags of character, plenty of space inside and out, very little else. Do you want to buy it?" she asked with obvious irony.

"Maybe we could share the burden? My meagre savings never seem to catch up with mortgage deposits, but might just repair the roof."

"Are you serious?" Vicky asked, somewhat astonished.

"Could be, yes. Between us we could restore it and write a book about the operation, text and photos. Plenty of interest in DIY projects, Vicky, so we should find a publisher O.K. Might even be able to interest T.V."

"Are you proposing a business partnership?"

"If that's all you want," Tom paused, then a smile lit up his face. "More fun to combine business with pleasure though, eh? More satisfactory all round."

"Much," Vicky conceded, returning his smile.

And they sealed the contract in a most suitable manner, witnessed by four dogs and one eccentric cat, conspirators all.

DRIVERS' WATERLOO

Road tax comes and road tax goes.
What it's spent on no one knows.
All Turbo drivers must despair,
Their road receives so little care.
From Broderick Falls to Eldoret,
Whether the weather's dry or wet,
You bump and bang, you slide and meander,
After the joys of a drive in Uganda.
You wonder: "Will my car get through?"
And why you drove, and why not flew,
Because though Kenya could certainly boast
A ghastly crop of the absolute most
Terrible roads you're likely to drive on,
You're now on the worst
And I hope you'll survive on
This stretch of the highway which really appals:
It's the main Eldoret through from Broderick Falls.

Machakos   1961

THE CHASTISEMENT OF HUBRIS

Andrew managed to keep his features expression-less, hiding his intense interest as Bertram's folder came under scrutiny. Bertram's face, Andrew noted, positively glowed with self congratulation as he proudly presented his course work for assessment.

Miss Mansfield beamed with unconcealed delight at the still-life of seashore flotsam. "It's charming, Bertram," she enthused, her eyes sparkling. "This piece alone might well earn you an A grade."

Andrew resisted a temptation to fidget as he surveyed the class, gauging the effect upon his peers of Bertram's nauseating smugness. He was preening like a bird of paradise, while Andrew barely concealed his contempt behind taut features, impatient for the coup-de-grace.

Five more pieces were examined, each one more highly praised.

As Miss Mansfield examined the seventh offering, her face underwent a monumental change. Colour rose to her cheeks then quickly drained away as embarrassment gave way to anger.

"How dare you!" she hissed through clenched teeth.

There before her was the image of a nude figure, a figure whose face bore an uncanny likeness to her own.

Bertram's mouth gaped, fishlike, his eyes starting from their sockets, for he had absolutely no knowledge of this drawing.

Andrew stroked his chin, in order to mask his smile of amused satisfaction as the class creeper received his comeuppance.

THOUGHTS OF HOME

Four thousand miles and more away
The leafy lanes of rural Kent
Call me now that summer's there.
The simple scenes of sun and shade
And greenness and a summer sky,
But most of all the pleasures shared
With friends with whom I feel at ease,
Are joys I miss this far from home.
How comfortable, how comforting
To share such pleasures with a friend.
A summer Sunday should be spent
In lazy, leafy lanes in Kent.

Finding today a lazy stream,
With trees beside and stones within,
There, as I sat, tears stung my eyes,
For I was lost, remembering.
Leaving my mortal form I flew
Across that space unbridgeable
And in imagination came
To rest by Woodstock Lanes in Kent.

Say that these pleasures only sleep
And will awaken once again,
For summer Sundays should be spent
In lazy, leafy lanes in Kent.

Machakos 1960

NGA KANOHI O TE RANGI

Having escaped to her dressing room at last, Kii surrendered to powerful emotions. She clutched a small spray of rata blossom and through tears which blurred her reflection, she glimpsed the child she had once been. Her thoughts carried her back in time, back twelve years, more than half her young life. She was eight years old.

*   *   *   *

Kii's father, Turi, farmed a few acres just north of Tairua on the east coast of the Coromandel Peninsular and fished the plentiful inshore waters of the mighty Pacific. Kii's three grown-up brothers had forsaken the land and the sea in pursuit of quicker gains in Auckland city. When the third one left home Kii sensed her father's disappointment. He was still sufficiently bound by Maoritanga to believe that without land a man was impoverished, no matter how much he might earn in the Pakeha's city. So Kii, the child of his mature years, became very close.

She accompanied her father on his fishing trips

when not at school and during these companionable days in the small boat Kii learnt much from Turi. He recounted many Maori legends and the heroic struggles of their ancestors, stories about the great migration to New Zealand - Aotearoa - Land of the Long White Cloud. He spoke to her in her mother tongue, instilling in her a love of her Maori heritage.

On one such occasion, soon after her grandfather's funeral tangi, she sat silently in the bow, baiting hooks.

"You're very quiet, little one. Why are you so thoughtful?"

"The tangi," Kii replied. "I was thinking about Granpa's goodbye."

"You mustn't let it trouble you, Kii. Taua had a good life, a long life. He was tired and it was time for his spirit to fly to Hawaiki. The time of mourning is over now."

"But is that all?" Kii asked. "Was he a Christian? Will he go to heaven?"

"First he was Maori. He believed that death of the body is final, but that his soul would fly to Hawaiki, our ancient homeland. Do you remember the story I told you, how Maui lost his contest with Hine-nui-te-po? She won the right to guard men's souls."

Tears glistened in Kii's eyes, and Turi held her hands, comforting her.

"All men die, Kii, but not their love. Their love goes on and helps us to live. Taua's spirit has flown to Hawaiki, but his love will watch over us from the stars, the eyes of the sky."

Turi drew from his pocket a small image, a Tiki carved from New Zealand jade, and placed it in Kii's hand. "This was my father's and his father's before that, and maybe his father's too. Take it Kii, it's yours now. Read what it says on the back and remember it; keep the Tiki and the thought inscribed on it as a talisman."

"Nga kanohi o te rangi," she read aloud. "The eyes of the sky. And will Taua's love really live there and watch over us?"

"I'm certain of it, and not just his love but all the love ever felt. If only the world believed it, then it would be a happier place. Love is the most powerful mana in the world. It can work miracles if we let it. It can help us do whatever we want with our lives."

Kii put her arms around her father's neck and hugged him.

* * * *

Returning to the present briefly, the memory of that day triggered other nostalgic thoughts, and she let her mind drift back in time, failing to notice a small card as it fell from the rata blossoms she still held.

In the early hours of her twelfth birthday she had awoken suddenly. It was the sort of still night when sounds travel great distances and the lapping of the waves on the shore came clearly to Kii. The cry of a gull broke the stillness, unmistakably echoing the sound of her name. Fascinated, she crept over to the window. The sky was lit by a million stars, for the moon had not yet risen. She listened for the gull to call again and was not disappointed: "Kii, Kii," as clearly as if - but she checked the thought too late, for it had already crossed her mind that it sounded like her father calling her; impossible, for Turi had been lost at sea a year earlier, his body never recovered.

The gull called once more and Kii strained forward, scanning the sky for sight of the bird. She dislodged her Tiki from the windowsill and it fell into the garden. Pulling on a pair of jeans and a sweater, Kii stole outside to retrieve it. She found it without difficulty and, as she stood, she saw the gull perched on the sill. It called just once and flew off toward the shore. Kii watched until it flew out of sight then, without thinking, she followed.

At the water's edge she sat, listening to the hypnotic wash of the waves caressing the rocks at her feet. The ocean, that sometimes awesome Pacific, was in friendly mood, befitting its name, and she felt its peaceful rhythm.

Her father had also loved the sea and the stars, the eyes of the sky by which he navigated. Kii felt that the sea must have loved him too, for hadn't it jealously taken him for itself and refused to deliver him up?

She was still musing on this thought when a gull landed beside her. It was much tamer than any she had seen before. She reached out a hand towards it and it stroked her fingers with its beak. Kii felt that the bird was trying to speak; ridiculous, of course, and yet?

Lifting its head, the gull looked out to sea, and Kii followed its gaze to where the winking lights of a small boat blinked, then disappeared. Or maybe they were stars set very close to the horizon? She could not be sure. When she looked back the bird had gone. On the rock was the greenstone Tiki which Kii picked up, idly reading the inscription though she knew it by heart. She didn't remember putting the token on the rock, but then she hardly remembered walking to the shore.

The moon was rising as Kii slowly made her way home. She felt happy, extraordinarily happy. An inexplicable feeling of contentment enveloped her. How beautiful the silvered ferns looked in the moonlight! As she walked beneath the Norfolk Island pines which cast their exploring shadows across her path, Kii thrust her hands into her pockets and froze, her heart pounding. Withdrawing her hands she stared in disbelief at the identical Tikis, one nestling in the palm of each hand. She had no memory of arriving home.

In the morning she woke with the sun's rays flooding her bed. She smiled contentedly as she basked in the sun's warmth, recalling the night's events as pleasant, if bewildering, dreams. Crossing to the window, she saw the twin Tikis on the sill and was momentarily paralysed. With an effort of will she reached out to touch both tokens. There really were two! And each bore the same Maori legend. When she had sufficiently calmed down, she wondered if her father really had sent her a second talisman, but how? Was Turi telling her, somehow, that he watched over her from the stars? She knew this made little sense, but she could think of no other explanation, however hard she tried.

She wrote a full account of the night's strange events for her school homework and was commended for her vivid imagination. How could she tell anyone it was all true without risking ridicule?

After the long summer holidays Kii started at the district high school. Her teachers soon recognised that she had special gifts, both creative and physical which, if channelled in the right direction, might lead to a career in dance. For her part, Kii found such delight in music and expressive movement that she worked tirelessly at it.

Kii wanted success, not just for herself but for her

father's memory and for all Maori children who felt themselves somehow inferior, unable to compete. She won a scholarship to an international ballet school where she displayed such magical qualities that her teachers predicted that it would be simply a matter of time before she found stardom.

* * * *

Back in her dressing-room, the haze had cleared from the looking glass and Kii's thoughts returned to the present. Time had indeed rewarded her dedication; she had found success and her tears were tears of joy and gratitude. The audience had loved her and, though she could not yet know it, the critics were preparing to write reviews full of superlatives, proclaiming a new star, a Maori Fonteyne. How proud Turi would be, for she was in no doubt that he knew.

She was still clasping the small spray of rata blossom and miniature fern fronds, so typical of her native New Zealand. She picked up the small card from the dressing-table. It was shaped like a Tiki and Kii knew what the message would be before she turned it over: *'Nga kanohi o te rangi'.*

Tears once more welled unbidden to her eyes, making the flowers swim out of focus. One might almost imagine them unreal, a figment of a vivid imagination; no more than that, maybe.

TO SUNSETS AND DAWNS

I've watched the sun go down from many skies,
And seen it sink below so many seas;
Then, span of darkness passed, I've watched it rise,
Splintering its rays through filtering trees.
From fair New Zealand skies I've seen its glow
Drawing vermilion clouds into a lake,
Or making Tasman's swell a painter's show;
Seen too, above Pacific clouds, dawn make
A pink and turquoise backdrop end the night.
The Kenyan sunsets, overflowing, paint
A second image to reflect their might.
You'd think that Britain's sunsets were too faint
To challenge those of more exotic skies,
But being those of home, they feast the eyes.

Seaford, Sussex 1972

JOSHUA'S BIG DAY

Joshua released the goats from the thornbrush pen and herded them away from the village and towards the common grazing grounds. Several other boys and girls of seven or eight were doing the same with their families' animals.

Joshua watched with envy as his two elder brothers and his eldest sister walked off in the opposite direction, neat in their green cotton uniforms, their books tied with sisal straps. How he wished he could go to school too! He longed to be able to read and learn about the big wide world beyond Ukambani. But his job was to herd the animals each day, until Amos was able to take over, and his father had enough shillings to buy his uniform and his books.

He waved to his brothers and sister. Then, kicking the red murram dust with his bare feet, he set off with the animals. He carried a small sisal bag and a water gourd slung around his neck.

Looking at the animals, he wondered why it was the sheep and goats looked so alike. Only the way the goats' tails stood upright could you tell the difference. He looked at the head-man's cattle, too. They were large white beasts with a few black spots. They had floppy humps above their shoulders and some had very long horns. His father didn't own any cattle for he was not a rich man.

Reaching the grazing land, he found a high rocky outcrop to sit on. From there he could see a long way and keep an eye on all his father's goats, making sure that none were lost. Jacob, his big brother, had taught him to count so that he could check the animals. From his rocky perch he looked out across the valley where, in the distance, he could see a few long-necked giraffes feeding on the acacia trees and a herd of zebras grazing nearby.

Joshua took out his prize possession — almost his only possession — a sharp little knife. He started to whittle away at a piece of wood, as he had seen the carvers doing at Wamunyu, where they made masks and many different animals for the tourists in Nairobi.

The thought of the tourists made him daydream about faraway places. Jacob had talked to him about many countries, some of them thousands of miles across the sea. But he wasn't even sure that he understood what the sea was! If only he could go to school, then he would know many things.

There was a droning in the sky and he looked up into the deep blue to see, very high up, an aeroplane. It looked so small, like a mosquito, but he knew that it was very big, for his brother had told him that all the people from his village could get inside it together! It was very hard to believe a thing like that. He watched it heading for Nairobi airport, leaving a thin white trail as it went.

Joshua had never been to Nairobi. Even his father

had been there only once, many years ago. The furthest Joshua had ever been was Machakos, the biggest township in Ukambani. It was a long day's walk away, even for grown-ups. There were many dukas there selling everything from maizeflour to school uniforms, and two garages, a post office and a big stone church. Most important of all, for Joshua, there was a High School and a Teachers' College. One day, if he attended primary and intermediate school, worked hard and passed his exams, he hoped to go to the High School in Machakos, but that was a long way off. Jacob would soon do his exams for the High School, after eight years' studying.

"Eight years!" Joshua thought. "That's all my life so far. I have a lot of work ahead of me."

"Joshua," one of his friends shouted to him, "one of your goats has strayed. See, it's over there by the trees."

Joshua thanked his friend and ran off towards the trees. He realised he'd been daydreaming, neglecting his animals. His father would be very angry indeed if he lost even the smallest kid. They had never seen lions this close to the village but rumour had it that a leopard sometimes visited that cluster of trees.

He shouted loudly and banged two sticks together as he followed the goat into the trees. If the leopard were close by that would frighten it away. They were fierce animals, Joshua knew, but they were shy, too and hid away during daylight hours. He caught the goat quickly and turned to go, but then he saw a bag beside a rough track at the edge of the trees. There was no-one about and when he called out, nobody answered.

"Who has left this here?" Joshua wondered. He looked inside where he found a camera and a notebook.

He didn't know it was a camera because he had never seen one before. "I'll take it to father," he decided. "He'll know what we must do."

Returning to his high rock he counted his goats, anxious to check that none of the others had strayed. He put the bag with his water gourd in a shady crevice in the rocks.

For the rest of the day he tried not to daydream but it was difficult because now he had something new to think about: the black box. He had no idea what it could be.

When the sun began to sink over the Mua Hills away to the west, the young herdsmen took up their gourds and herded the animals onto the homeward path. Joshua hung the gourd strap around his neck, placed the new bag inside his sisal one and made his way home.

His father was sitting in the doorway, drinking maize beer with the village head-man. After penning the goats Joshua approached them.

"Father, I found a bag today, near the grazing land. It has a strange black box inside and a book."

His father took the bag and opened it. The head-man saw the box as it was taken from the bag.

"This is a picture making box, I think," he said. "We must not open it. My son showed me a picture of one in a paper. Very clever boxes, all the white people have them, so he says. They make pictures of animals and people."

The next day Joshua's younger brother, Amos, and his sister Mary were sent off to tend the goats while Joshua's father took him to the police post at Wamunyu to hand in the bag.

The sergeant inspected the bag and its contents.

"Where did you find this, boy?" he asked.

So Joshua described the place carefully. Then the sergeant spoke into a machine. When he returned Joshua was amazed to learn that he had spoken to an officer in Machakos, so far away. Oh how he wanted to learn all about these wonderful machines and so much more!

"It's good you found this bag. A newspaper man lost it and you are in luck. He promised 500 shillings reward to anyone who returned his camera. I hope no-one opened it and spoiled the pictures."

"500 shillings?" Joshua marvelled. "How many books will that buy?"

The journalist drove to Wamunyu to collect his belongings and to pay the reward, then, what joy, he took Joshua and his father back to the village in his land-rover. Joshua felt very important.

For the next week Amos went with Joshua to tend the goats. He was a year and a half younger than Joshua but he was good with the animals. He learned quickly, as Joshua told their father that evening, after they had penned the goats.

"Very good," said their father. "That's what I needed to hear. From next week Amos will herd the goats. You will go to school with Jacob, Adam and Lizzie."

Joshua was overjoyed. He thanked his father and ran off happily to the boys' hut to tell Amos the news. He stopped in the doorway when he saw the new green shirt and shorts laid out on his sleeping mat. Excitedly, he tried them on, realising that some of the reward money had made this possible. Amos was pleased, too, for it meant that he now had a responsible job looking after the family's valuable animals.

On Monday Joshua waved to Amos and the other young boys herding the animals away from the village. He set off proudly with the older children, knowing that he was starting out on a great adventure, dressed in his new uniform. His big day had come at last.

THE KEY TO HARMONY

The key was missing.

"Well who the devil had it last?" Mr Means asked in a belligerent manner. "Tracy?"

"Don't look at me," the young filing clerk replied, all injured innocence. "I 'avent seen it since yesterday morning."

Mr Means drummed his fingers impatiently against the offending filing cabinet. "Turn out your handbag," he ordered in a voice redolent of the gestapo.

No sign of the key.

"'ow about your pockets?" young Tracy dared to propose.

Mr Means blustered, his blood pressure rising dangerously. "Are you suggesting that I'm responsible for losing it?" he accused her, in his most pompous tone.

"Well, you use it too, don't you?" Tracy countered cheekily.

"How dare you! Much more of your insolence and I'll report you to Mr Brennan, young lady." His voice remained threatening, like a bullying schoolmaster's. His face was suffused with unsightly purple blotches.

Tracy laughed; sniggered really. "Go on like that and you'll give yourself an 'eart attack," she jeered, like a disruptive schoolgirl.

That did it. He lunged at the girl, losing control completely.

Tracy side-stepped neatly and he fell heavily against his own desk, scattering papers, pens, phone — the lot. There among the debris shone the missing key.

APPOINTMENT WITH CHARON

The day must come, in spite of care,
when she must leave, no time to spare,
for none can stay that final sleep
when our appointed hour we keep
and Ferryman collects his fare.

At ninety-two she's passed the bare
allotted three-score-ten; her share
outruns the norm, but Death will reap.
The day must come.

My Mother's life runs out.   Her chair
faces the sea. She views the fair
extent of Seaford Bay's curving sweep.
Her family, so large, will weep
some when she dies, but not despair.
The day must come.

In memory of Rose Evelyn Barfoot 1903 - 1998

Seaford, Sussex 1995

JUST THE TICKET

"Gran! Gran, I'm here — late again."
The back door stood wide open. Kenny was surprised for it was extremely cold that November. He went into the kitchen and called again: no answer. In the living-room he stood frozen with shock. Gran's neat little room was a complete shambles: drawers emptied everywhere, the china cabinet - gran's pride and joy - was ransacked and the place was littered with feathers from a slashed cushion.

"Gran!" he yelled, charging up the stairs. The bedroom was in the same terrible state and on the floor, amidst the chaos, lay Kenny's grandmother, battered into unconsciousness.

Kenny knelt beside her, feelings of rage, anxiety and disbelief warring inside him. He felt her neck and found a weak pulse. Dragging a blanket from the bed he tucked it round the frail form.

"You'll be O.K. Gran. Shan't be a mo." He raced across the street to a neighbour and hammered on the door, yelling at the top of his voice.

"What a racket! Kenny, whatever's up?" Mrs Jackson asked.

"Gran's been beat up. Phone, need to phone." And he pushed past to the phone in the hallway. Mrs Jackson listened open mouthed as the lad phoned 999, coping well with the emergency. She followed him back to his gran, and once in the bedroom was shocked but practical. "Better not move her," she advised. "Might be something broken."

So Kenny knelt beside his grandmother, holding her hand, speaking words of comfort which she was unable to hear. Tears streaked his face as he looked at her bruised and battered form.

"I'm sorry, Gran. If I hadn't been kept in — How could anyone? She never hurt no-one and she didn't have nothing worth stealing. I'll get the bastards."

Kenny realised that if this had happened any day but Wednesday he would not have gone to Empire Terrace and his gran could have lain undiscovered until it was too late. He feared it might already be too late. He regretted the ten minutes spent smoking a fag in Jubilee Park. Could he have prevented this mugging but for that cigarette?

Boys of fourteen are seldom credited with any finer feelings, particularly when they are inclined to mischief, as Kenny was, but his gran meant a lot to him and now he felt guilty.

"There's the ambulance," Mrs Jackson said. "I'll let them in."

The paramedics fitted a collar as a precaution before carrying Gran to the ambulance. Kenny left his bike in the yard and went with them. When they'd gone, Mrs Jackson folded the blanket, putting it on the bed, then phoned Kenny's mum and spoke to the police who arrived soon after the ambulance drove away.

After Gran was settled in the ward, Kenny and his mother sat at her bedside, anxious to be there when she woke. Detective Sergeant Brent was there too. Gran looked battered and ill and seemed to have aged suddenly. Apart from the bruises and black eyes, a broken arm had been pinned, ribs strapped and forty stitches bore witness to the savagery of the attack. Later, when Gran had woken up and taken a few sips of water, the Sergeant asked the ward sister's permission to ask some questions.

She hesitated, then reluctantly agreed: "Just one or two; she's very poorly and may recall very little at present."

"Mrs Neeves, do you know the people who attacked you?" he asked several times. Gran was so doped up that she hardly heard the question, never mind understanding it. Through the haze in her head she saw Kenny's face and whispered his name.

"I'm here, Gran. You'll be O.K. now. You're safe now."

Meanwhile the sergeant was busy adding two and two and making five. "Now young man," he said. "You can answer a few questions."

"Course, anything to help nick the blokes that done it."

"How come you were at your grandmother's this afternoon?"

"I always go on Wednesdays. I go straight from school and have my tea there."

"And what time does school finish?"

"Half past three, but I didn't get out till four o'clock — kept in again."

The sergeant raised a cynical eyebrow: "What did you do then?"

"Got my bike and went to Gran's. I was late see, so I went straight there. Good job I did too. Gran could've died there all on her own, couldn't she?"

"What time did you get to your grandmother's house?"

"I dunno, I didn't look. I suppose it was about ten past four most likely. I was only there two minutes before I phoned emergency."

"I'll check how long you were kept at school, of course," the sergeant warned.

Kenny was, in his own words, gobsmacked. True, Gran had whispered his name, but only because she could see him. "Yes, O.K. Mr Phillips kept me in, found us smoking behind the gym when he was on duty. Half an hour he kept me, a bit longer than the others — for cheek, he said. What you asking me all this for? Why don't you go out and pick up the bast... the men who beat up my gran?"

His mother chided him for his rudeness.

"That's all right, Mrs Gale. We're used to it. As for you, lad, watch yourself. I shall want to see you again tomorrow."

"Why? What for?"

"To take your written statement, lad. O.K.?" With that the sergeant left the hospital.

At midnight the sister advised Kenny's mum that they should go home. Gran was sleeping soundly and Kenny had to be up at six-thirty for his paper round, so they left her, knowing she was in good hands.

Kenny finished his paper round in good time, running all the way, then ran on to Empire Terrace. Mrs Jackson had locked up after the police left and Kenny took the key from under the geranium pot and let himself in the back door. The state of the place still appalled him. He'd only come for his bike and wasn't sure why he went inside, habit maybe, disbelief, or intuition even? He looked in the living-room for anything which didn't belong there, but found nothing. He found gran's clock, smashed of course, under a cushion, stopped at four-twenty. It threw him until he remembered it was always kept twenty minutes fast. So, it had stopped at four o'clock exactly.

He looked in the bedroom but found nothing that did not belong there either. He picked up the blanket and shook it out, intending to spread it over the bed, but his attention was caught by a small piece of paper which dropped out of it. He picked it up to examine it: a bus ticket, folded in a complicated way. Kenny opened it out: *service 14, farestage 11, Wednesday 20th November, 95 pence.* As he released one edge the tight folds re-formed. He put it in his pocket, thoughtfully, locked up and went off to school, collecting his bike from the yard.

At dinner time Sergeant Brent visited the school to check with Mr Phillips and to take Kenny's statement.

"Who knew you were going to be late getting to your gran's?" the Sergeant asked.

"All me mates knew, I suppose."

"And your enemies? Have you got enemies?"

"No, I don't go in for enemies. What's all this about anyway?"

"Just getting a few background details."

Mr Phillips confirmed that Kenny appeared to have no enemies. "He's very popular with all the pupils as a rule, the court jester."

Kenny wasn't sure whether or not to feel insulted by this, but Mr Phillips was smiling, so he let it go.

"I checked with the operator; it was four-twenty

when you phoned the emergency service. Twenty minutes to cycle just over a mile?"

"I told you. I didn't look at the time. I was too busy. Anyway, Gran was mugged at four. Her clock — " Kenny realised he had said too much.

"As you were saying — her clock? What about it , lad? You were too busy to notice the time, remember?"

"Yes. Well, I didn't notice it yesterday. It was this morning."

"This morning? You went to the house this morning? Why?"

"My bike. I had to fetch my bike from the yard."

"You'll be telling me next that the clock was in the yard." The sergeant's sarcasm expressed his disbelief.

"'Course not. I don't know why I went in, but I did. Gran's clock was smashed at four o'clock. It said four-twenty, but Gran always kept it twenty minutes fast. She hated being late anywhere."

"Back to the point. If you went straight to your grandmother's why didn't you phone until four-twenty, twenty minutes after you were let out of school. Why?"

"It must've taken me longer than I thought to get my bike from the sheds and leave school. I don't know."

The sergeant leaned over Kenny. "You don't seem to know much, lad. You'd better start remembering. Maybe you spent some time at the house. Doing what?"

"No, I didn't. I didn't! I went across to Mrs Jackson's as soon as I found Gran and tucked the blanket round. What you getting at?"

"Well now, something doesn't add up. We seem to have lost a few minutes somewhere." The Sergeant paused. "Well?"

"All right then!" Kenny ran a hand through his hair.

"I stopped for a cigarette. Gran thinks I've chucked it, so I can't smoke at her house. I had one in the park, on the way there."

Mr Phillips was shaking his head and the Sergeant wore that cynical look, again.

"That's the truth," Kenny blurted. "Ask Darren Leach, he was there with me."

"And why couldn't you have told me before?"

"I felt guilty. I could've got to Gran's sooner if I hadn't had a fag."

"So is that it now? Anything else I should know before I leave?"

Kenny hesitated a moment. "Nothing else," he said, having decided not to tell Sergeant Brent about the bus ticket because he was narked by his attitude, and anyway, he wanted to check it out for himself. He knew the number fourteen passed not far behind Gran's road, but it wasn't the service she used. The number six passed the end of her street.

After school Kenny went to the bus station to check out the ticket. "King's Head on Fairly Street. Twenty minutes to the hour, twenty to six in the morning till midnight," he was told.

The bus stop was deserted by the time Kenny got there, of course; the twenty-to-four had long gone. He looked around the area to find, apart from the pub, some seedy looking shops, a few run-down houses and a couple of small factories. "What next?" he wondered, realising he was no Columbo.

The following day Kenny dashed from school the moment his class was dismissed. He ran full pelt all the way to the King's Head and scrambled aboard the bus as it was leaving.

He slumped onto a seat, breathing hard. Having

recovered his breath, he looked around, sizing up his fellow passengers: a couple of housewives with bulging shopping bags occupied the seat by the door, opposite them sat a frail old man in an army great-coat several sizes too big for him, while at the back a gaggle of primary kids squirmed in their seats like a litter of puppies.

Kenny dismissed all his fellow travellers immediately. The mugger was not on the bus, so Kenny left it at the next stop, feeling let down. Had he really expected to see and, what's more, recognise his gran's attacker? He wasn't sure what he had expected to find but he still felt disappointed. He was tempted to throw away the folded ticket, but the memory of Gran's battered face made him hang on to it. "Keep it. Give it some more thought," he decided, making his way back to school to collect his bike.

He was pleased to see his gran looking a lot better that evening, in spite of the unsightly bruising and stitches. She was wearing a smart new bed-jacket which his mum had brought in that morning.

"A man from the telly came this afternoon. I can't think why anyone would be interested to see me in this state. What a sight!"

Kenny wondered at her powers of recovery. She always said her generation was tough. She was right! "There was a police sergeant came, too. You'll never believe it, he asked me if you and your pals had done it! I told him he must be daft. I gave him a description, too: reddish hair, one gold ear-ring, quite tall, as tall as your dad, but a lot younger, only about nineteen or twenty I should guess," Kenny's gran concluded.

In bed that night Kenny got his brain in gear and

looked at the facts. Wednesday, he'd wait till Wednesday and get that bus again. Maybe the bloke's habits changed on Wednesdays, or maybe he wasn't a regular on the number fourteen. It needed checking.

On Wednesday he was careful to behave himself at school as he couldn't risk being kept in. He considered playing truant but thought better of it. He patiently bore the sarcasm of Miss Dodds regarding the accuracy of his history homework, maintaining a stoical silence with difficulty. In art he took some stick, too. He told Mr Newman he would spoil his drawing if he painted it, and he did. Some folk were never satisfied. At break he refused a cigarette and remained aloof all day, quite out of character. Thus, at three-forty he boarded the bus outside the King's Head, having padlocked his bike to some railings.

His scalp tingled as he saw a young red-haired man board the bus and sit just across the gangway from him: about five feet eleven, maybe twenty years old. Kenny felt sure he had found Gran's attacker. He realised he was sweating, in spite of the cold day, and he tried not to seem too interested. He looked away, feeling his heart thumping against his ribs. What now? He tried to appear casual as he looked back, checking the single ear-ring. It was him right enough.

The man turned his head and stared right at Kenny who found himself looking into the palest eyes he had ever seen, almost colourless they were, hard and icy, and they seemed to bore right through Kenny's skull. With an effort he looked away, hoping that he was maintaining an impassive expression. He had intended following the man off the bus, but he now knew he was out of his depth. He had to tell the police.

Out of the corner of his eye he could see the man's

fingers fidgeting with something. They were busily folding his bus ticket. The hairs on the back of Kenny's neck rose and prickled; his heart quickened. If he had needed confirmation that was it. This was the bastard who'd beaten up his gran for a few quid.

As the mugger rose, Kenny looked up and made eye contact. The cold pale eyes held him, mesmerised. The man leaned down and grasped the front of Kenny's anorak. "You'll know me again, squirt, next time you see me," the redhead said, and he pushed Kenny away roughly. As he left the bus he dropped his ticket in the gangway.

Kenny recovered his composure, noted the bus stop and pocketed the discarded ticket. "Yes," he thought. "I'll know you again, you bastard." Now he had two tickets to show that suspicious Sergeant.

Det. Sgt. Brent was not best pleased with Kenny for withholding the first ticket, but he had Mrs Neeves' description of her attacker and the boy appeared to have found a likely suspect. At last he had a lead.

A constable came into the sergeant's office with a message then and noticed the twin tickets on the desk. "Are you taking up book-crafts, Sarge?" he asked with a grin.

"Book-crafts? What are you on about, Gibson?"

"Them. As expertly folded a pair of right-angled gussets as ever I saw," the constable replied pompously.

"Say that again." And he did.

"Explain."

"Well Sarge, before I joined the force I worked at a small cardboard file manufacturers. The expanding gussets in the best files had corners just like those."

"And where was that, Constable?"

"Off Fairly Street, near the King's Head. Thompson and Brown."

A phone call confirmed that the factory still existed: "Eight-thirty till five pm, three-thirty on Wednesdays because of football training," Sergeant Brent was told. It did not take long to organise the necessary back-up, and Kenny was taken along for the ride, though he was not allowed out of the car at the factory.

The following afternoon Mrs Neeves was in good spirits when Kenny visited her. "Hello, Kenny love, you're a bit of a hero, it seems. Are you going to be a detective when you grow up?"

"Not me," Kenny replied. "That job makes people too suspicious minded. Anyway, who's been talking?"

"That sergeant's been in. Quite a nice young man, really. He didn't have to come."

"No, I suppose not. What did he say?"

"He told me how you'd tracked down the mugger and how they'd got him locked up. He gave you a lot of credit, too."

"He's changed his tune. He was not too pleased when I gave him the bus tickets. Blew his stack, he did. Anyhow, that redhead left a perfect set of dabs on your wardrobe door so there's plenty of evidence to put him away for a fair while. The sergeant reckons he'll have a hard time in jail 'cos most cons don't take kindly to jokers who beat up old ladies or little kids. Serve him right, too."

Kenny's mother arrived then, looking rather pleased with herself.

"Hello, Mum," Mrs Gale said, bending over to plant a kiss on her mother's bruised cheek. "You're looking very cheerful. I can see you're feeling much better."

"I certainly am now they've got him, the vicious devil, and all thanks to Kenny, so the sergeant says."

"Yes, and that's not all. I've brought some more good news. Jack and I have talked it all through. We want you to come and live with us when you leave hospital. If you want to, of course."

"Oh yes, Gran!" Kenny exclaimed. "That's just the ticket!"

And so it was, just in time for Christmas, too.

THE PORTRAIT

Mary didn't mind the delayed take-off; it served to heighten her anticipation. She sat in the window seat watching the novelty of airport activity.

Across the gangway Senor Gonzales again searched his memory. He had seen her before, but where? For the life of him he could not remember. He was sure he knew that oval face, the generous mouth, the flyaway eyebrows and, most of all, the eyes, blue-black eyes, and jet black hair gently curling at the nape of the slender neck.

A fleeting expression as she turned her head rang a tantalising bell of recognition, but it soon escaped. He then noticed her hand as she pushed back a strand of hair from her forehead. Yes, even the hand's sensitive fingers seemed familiar. His eyes narrowed beneath greying brows in an effort to place her in another setting.

Earlier, in the departure lounge, he had read the label on her cabin bag: '*Mary Benson, Puerto de Soller via Palma, Mallorca*'. The name was English yet she did not look typically English. Anyway, the name meant nothing to the Senor, but he was intrigued by the native spelling of his island home. Most tourists seemed not to know it and certainly never used it.

The Captain made a short announcement. The seatbelt signs lit up and they were under way. Mary Benson's eyes did not leave the window as she watched the airport receding and the patchwork of the Sussex countryside unfolding beneath them. This was obviously her first flight and her excitement was plain. Once they had risen above the clouds she at last sat back in her seat and relaxed just a little. Bernado Gonzales also relaxed, convinced by now that his efforts to place Mary were simply a case of wishful thinking!

As the plane approached Palma airport, Mary leant forward, straining against the seat belt, her eyes searching the land she already loved yet had never seen.

Since she first encountered the island in a travel book two years earlier she had known that she would love Mallorca. For those two long years she had saved from a meagre wage, spurred on by this obsession, and now she looked forward to three whole weeks in heaven! She knew she would regret none of the sacrifices she had made to pay a little more for a private holiday, having formed her idea of package holidays from some unfavourable press reports.

As they taxied along the runway, she saw the windmills as familiar sights, for she had read about them. Their presence, so close at hand, gave substance to her arrival. She had made it.

She waited in vain at the carousel for her luggage. Her brand new suitcase was nowhere to be seen.

Senor Gonzales noticed that she looked bewildered.

"Excuse me," he said in barely accented English. "You have a problem?"

"My case is not here."

"Indeed, that is a problem. Wait here while I make enquiries."

He sought the baggage handlers who assured him that everything had been unloaded. He then reported the loss and was assured that the matter would be speedily dealt with.

"Your case, I'm sorry to say, must still be at Gatwick, but the hostess assures me that it will be here for you tomorrow. I'm so sorry. Is there anything you need for tonight?"

Tears prickled Mary's eyes: "No, thank you, I can manage tonight," she told him. But she wondered if it was all going wrong so soon.

"Then I'll tell you what we shall do. If you'll allow me, I'll drive to Puerto de Soller in the morning and bring you to Palma to collect your case. How's that?"

"That would be very kind of you, but ..."

"Then no buts. I live at Lluc Alcari, not far from Soller. It will be a pleasure. Allow me to introduce myself, Bernado Gonzales."

"Benson, Mary Benson." He shepherded her towards the exit, where the duty policeman saluted, addressing him by name.

"Good. There's the car," he said. "Poor Miguel, my brother must have had quite a wait."

Mary was introduced to Miguel, whose disarming smile seemed familiar. His easy welcome banished her feelings of disappointment and she momentarily forgot the wayward suitcase.

Even the early part of the journey, across the flatness of the plain, Mary enjoyed but as the car sped toward the mountain road, through olive groves, she bubbled with unconcealed delight. She loved the gnarled old trees, their sinuous writhings a witness to their struggle for survival over many centuries. "They're fantastic," she remarked, "but so beautiful."

"Some of the trees are said to be more than a thousand years old. Just imagine the changes they have seen," Bernado remarked, and through the childlike wonder and delight in her eyes, he saw the trees anew, and he too found them beautiful. He never tired of returning to Mallorca.

By the time they had negotiated the snaking bends to the top of the mountain road it was twilight. Mary looked back at the distant lights peppering the city of Palma and felt at home.

It was quite dark by the time they reached Puerto de Soller and the lights skirting the bay etched a perfect arc. The lighthouse winked a friendly welcome and everything felt so comforting to Mary.

Miguel bade her goodnight and Bernado accompanied her into the hotel. "Are you sure you can manage for tonight?" he asked.

"Yes, thank you. Thank you for all your kindness," she replied.

"A pleasure. About eleven tomorrow? We can lunch in Palma and have a look round, if you would like to. Goodnight, Mary."

Having registered at reception, Mary was shown to a room which had a balcony overlooking the bay. She smiled wryly as she remembered she had so little to unpack. "What a beginning to my long awaited holiday!" she thought. She collected her toiletries from her cabin bag and, determined not to feel unhappy, declared: "I've arrived, haven't I?" as she enjoyed her shower.

She woke early and the brightness drew her onto

the balcony where she looked out upon the sparkling waters of the bay. "It's true!" she told the world. "At last I'm in Mallorca."

The sound of laughter and splashing water rose from the shore and Mary dressed hurriedly, ate a sketchy breakfast and went to inspect the local shops. Almost at once she returned to the hotel with a bikini which she quickly put on before running down to the narrow beach.

The water, the sun, the sky, the whole world was so delightful that Mary lost all sense of time. When she remembered, it was almost eleven. As she returned to the hotel the Gonzales' car drew up.

"Good morning, Mary Benson," Miguel greeted her, much to her surprise, for she had expected to see Bernado.

Her first impression of Miguel was confirmed as he walked over to her. "Good morning," she replied. "I'm sorry, I lost sight of the time. Where is Bernado?"

"He sends his apologies and asks that you look kindly on me as his substitute."

How could she do otherwise when he smiled so warmly? "Of course. I won't be long tidying up," Mary answered as she skipped up the steps into the hotel.

Driving to Palma was fun, for Miguel had an easy going manner and Mary soon relaxed. They made directly for the airport where they learned that the case would not arrive until 3 o'clock.

"Good!" Miguel exclaimed. "Then we have three hours to fill. I suggest we find a pleasant place to have an early lunch before exploring the city. Plenty of time to find the most picturesque back lanes. You'll like them, I'm sure."

Miguel appeared to be well known at the small restaurant where Mary enjoyed her first authentic paella. Afterwards, as promised, they wandered through the delightful narrow lanes of the old city, where the tall houses shut out the direct rays of the sun, keeping them cool in the heat of the day. Some had small balconies with hanging flower baskets, and in one lane opposite houses were joined by an archway which formed a small room. Mary was pleased her camera had been in her cabin bag.

An elderly woman was sitting beside a florist's doorway and when they stopped to admire the flowers she caught Mary's hand in her own, speaking a few words of Mallorquin to her. Miguel thanked the old woman and bought a spray of her gardenias before they passed on. As he fixed the flowers to Mary's dress he said: "They should go in your hair but it might look a lttle too exotic at this hour."

"What did the flower seller say?" Mary asked him.

"She said she was glad you had come home. Poor old thing, she's almost blind. She's mistaken you for someone else, no doubt."

But Mary did not dismiss the words so lightly. She did feel that she had come home. Her old guide books surely weren't responsible for the familiarity of the sights she kept encountering.

In the cool vastness of the impressive cathedral the old woman's words continued to sing, and Mary longed for them to be true.

She was lost in thought when Miguel touched her arm: "We should be heading for the airport," he said quietly.

Having collected the errant case they drove out

towards the mountain road. Mary was silent, still mulling over the old woman's words.

"Why so quiet?" she was asked.

"Sorry, I was dreaming; not very sociable of me," she replied.

"We're almost at the crest. Would you like to stop for a drink?"

"That would be very welcome. The paella was excellent but it has left me with a mammoth thirst."

When Miguel parked the car he did not get out at once. "Maria," he said, "may I call you Maria? I don't want to be a nuisance but, if you haven't planned every moment of your holiday, may I see you again?"

She smiled, and her eyes smiled too. "Nothing is planned. I came to explore."

"Wouldn't it be better to have a local guide?"

"It would be perfect," she admitted.

"Wonderful! It's time I took a holiday, and it's possible now that Bernado is home for a while. I'm at your service, for as long as you wish. How long are you staying?"

"Three weeks. Three sun-drenched weeks. Can you stand that?"

"It will be a pleasure, and I'm sure I shall return to my painting with renewed enthusiasm."

The days flew by, but they were full, happy days. Miguel took Mary to the glorious sands of Formentor, where they lazed in the sun and swam in the turquoise sea. They visited the beautiful Blue Gorge, the spectacular Caves of Drac, and saw the monastery where Chopin and George Sand had stayed. Mary was enchanted by this island of contrasts, especially the small sheltered bays and the wild mountains. She enjoyed wandering through orange groves, their walks among the hills girdling Fornalutx and their picnic on the slopes of Puig Major. In the evenings they sampled the night spot cabarets, the folk dancing and the flamenco, the sophistication of Tito's and the intimacy of The Patio. Miguel delighted in the enthusiasm and pleasure with which Mary approached each fresh experience.

"Today we are going to picnic in the Torrente de Pareis. I have the food and the wine; you will need your swimsuit and perhaps your camera. I hope you are a good sailor because we are going to forsake the roads and take to the sea."

"Wonderful!" Mary exclaimed, with customary eagerness. "I've been longing to see the coastline from the sea."

They chugged out of the horse shoe bay into the open sea, with an uninterrupted view from their vantage point atop the cabin of the Santa Rosa. Mary's eyes held a new, even more intense brightness as she watched the rugged coastline and the changing colours of the sea.

Miguel, who had seen it all before but still found it compelling, looked at Mary and, for the first time in his life, wanted to paint a portrait. He knew exactly how it would be: the head half turned to show the nape of the neck as it curved gently from the shoulders, the chin lifted to emphasize the joy in living, and the eyes - the eyes must be alive and full of wonder. "I want to paint you," he said, his thoughts finding a voice of their own.

Mary laughed. "I should never be able to keep still! You should paint all this," she said, gesturing at the magnificent cliffs, "and the fantastic olive trees."

"I have," he replied seriously. "Now I want to paint you, Maria. May I?"

"If you really want to, Miguel, but I don't know why."

He took her hand, and together they tried to read the signs in the inky depths around them and in the ancient cliffs which rose sheer from those same vast depths towards the cloudless sky. Mary thought how apt was the idea of the sea as the mystic element.

As the small boat was rounding the headland, Mary experienced a flash of insight into what she was about to see. Afterwards she could not be sure that the narrow cleft of the Torrente, the intersecting promontory and the tiny bay of La Calobra had really appeared to her a split second before they actually came into view. It was impossible, and yet she felt that she had known exactly what to expect. It was a strange, disquieting experience.

"Oh Miguel, this is truly magnificent, the best of so many wonderful places we've seen." And indeed it was a masterpiece of nature set against the awe inspiring backdrop of the mountains.

Miguel had expected her to like the place but he found her joy and enthusiasm infectious. He realised he might well be falling in love with her, or was he in love with her love of life itself?

The Santa Rosa tied up at the small quay which appeared to spring from the rocks. While the other passengers waited patiently to step ashore, Miguel leapt onto the quay from the deck . "Jump!" he called out. "I'll help you."

They were quickly onto the beach and soon reached the promontory separating La Calobra from the Torrente de Pareis. Mary was busy with her camera so Miguel took her beach bag. "I want to take a shot looking through the opening in the tunnel," she explained. But they had not yet reached the pedestrian tunnel cutting through the cliff on its way to the gorge.

"How do you know about the opening in the tunnel?" he asked.

It was yet another odd sensation. Mary felt her heart miss a beat and her bewildered expression disturbed Miguel. "Maybe I've read about it, or seen it on a postcard," she replied with a casualness she did not exactly feel. They both knew the incident could not be so easily explained.

When they emerged into the fierce sunlight they were facing the gorge in all its shimmering splendour. It snaked inland, a deep cleft cut through cliffs by centuries of raging torrents. The watercourse was dry at that season and coarse grass and scrubby bushes sprang from its bed. Further up the gorge the rock walls rose sheer and, in the illusion of disappearing perspective, seemed to lean closer toward each other as they reached for the sky. Pine and wild fig trees dug their roots deeply into the fissures in the cliffs, grimly hanging on to life. The lower rocks were beautifully figured in intricate designs caused by erosion. Mary was lost for words as she absorbed these familiar sights, buried until now in her subconscious memory.

"You look as though you'd seen a ghost." Miguel's voice was little more than a whisper as he smiled and took her hand.

With an effort she dragged herself back to the present and, with a strained laugh, replied: "Maybe I have".

He squeezed her hand, wanting to reassure her, conscious that her laugh hid signs of the confusion within her. "Let's swim first, then we can take our picnic way up the gorge and find some shade," he suggested. Splashing around in the water, diving from the rocks, laughing for the sheer pleasure of laughter, Mary temporarily escaped from the unexplained familiarity of her surroundings and lost the bewildered expression Miguel had noticed earlier.

Hand in hand they walked slowly up the gorge, past the little shaded pools stranded after the winter torrent, and found a cool spot to picnic. They sat in the shade of a huge boulder which almost dammed the watercourse, and Mary thought what an awesome sight it must be when the rushing water swirled around it and cascaded over the top.

The wine and the heat made them drowsy and they talked quietly, in keeping with the tranquil scene. Each learned something of the other's past and shared a little of their hopes for the future.

"I'm very lucky to have a brother who thinks I have talent," Miguel confided, "otherwise I should make a poor living as a painter. Bernado runs the property business in Palma and London, while I give an eye to the estate and so find time to paint. He's very good to me, my brother, he even led me to you."

"I like him, but he seems - I don't know, lonely somehow."

"He is, at present. His wife died less than a year ago, and he works too hard, trying to fill the void. They were very close. Do you know, he still brings back presents from London, presents which he could intend only for her. He cannot accept the fact that she will not be at home, waiting for him."

"Yet he is so considerate with everybody. He was very kind to me. He need not have bothered."

"I'm so glad he did. But he's like that. I'm surprised he's such a good businessman; the two aspects seem incompatible."

"Why didn't he come, that first day, to take me to Palma?"

Miguel laughed. "Because I persuaded him he had an urgent appointment. Did you mind?"

"Who's fishing for compliments? You know I didn't. I've enjoyed it. It hasn't been too boring for you, has it?"

"Absolute servitude! I've enjoyed every minute of my slavery, and there aren't that many minutes left." He was serious suddenly, his eyes holding hers, seeing in them the same emptiness he felt at the thought of her imminent return to England.

"Don't let's waste them, then," her eyes seemed to say, and he kissed her, knowing that he had wanted to do so almost from the moment they had met. Her childlike innocence had blinded him, had made him consider her as a lovable child, to be carefully protected. Now he saw her as a woman, as the woman he loved and wanted to cherish.

On the return journey, as the Santa Rosa nosed out of the bay, the sight of the evening sun bathing the mountains behind La Calobra proved too much for Mary. Miguel saw the tears well up and escape, running down her tanned cheeks, and knew that he loved her. How had it taken him so long to realise it?

"Hasta luego," he whispered. "It's not goodbye. We'll be back."

Mary smiled bravely as she nestled against him, feeling the comfort of his arm around her shoulders. She dared not hope.

That evening, as they climbed the steep road past the lighthouse to the wooded clifftop of Cap Gros, they each wore a wistful sadness.

"Do you really have to leave on Sunday? Couldn't you stay for one more week?"

"You know how much I should like to, but there's my job and . ."

"Send them a cable. Word it '*Unable to return due to urgent business*'. It is urgent, Maria, very urgent, because I can't lose you now. Stay, querida mia, stay here and marry me."

At that moment a strong wind arose, accompanied by a flash of lightning and a simultaneous clap of thunder. The heavens opened, drenching them in seconds. The mood was shattered.

Miguel grabbed Mary's hand as they both ran for cover beneath some pine trees.

Mary was shivering, and not simply because of the cold. The suddenness of the storm at that precise moment terrified her. She saw it as an ill omen. The series of strange incidents since arriving in Mallorca had subconsciously played on her mind and the storm, coming when it did, seemed to be the confirmation of impending madness.

"Maria, we must get to the hotel quickly, dry off and warm ourselves. You're so cold. Let's go."

Once inside the warmth and light of the hotel, Mary's fears seemed less real, but she still felt unsure of herself.

Had she imagined that Miguel had proposed marriage? Had it been wishful thinking on her part? She could hardly ask Miguel. He ordered hot soup to be taken to Mary's room and she went up to change out of her wet clothes.

"I'll be here early tomorrow," Miguel promised, taking his leave.

By eleven the following morning there was no sign of Miguel and Mary was convinced he would not come. "He regrets his rash proposal," she thought, "if indeed it was a proposal!" She made a start on her packing, to occupy herself, for the next day she was due to return home.

Before lunch she took a walk around the local shops, buying presents for her mother and her friends. She felt flat, wondering how much of the past three weeks was simply imagined. When she returned to the hotel he was there, waiting for her in the bar and he greeted her as though nothing untoward had happened.

"How was your night?" he asked. "Did you have a good sleep?"

"Very good," she replied. "I was up in good time, ready for you."

"I'm sorry. As I explained, we had a bit of a panic this morning."

"Panic? I don't understand," Mary said.

"I left a message. I phoned early, to apologise, to say I'd be late."

Mary smiled, reassured.

"You didn't get my message, did you? Whatever did you think?"

"Never mind that, Miguel. What was the panic about?"

"An estate worker hurt himself quite badly falling off a ladder, so I drove him to the hospital. He's going to be fine," he explained.

"I've signed you out," he continued. "There's a room all ready for you at Lluc Alcari."

Mary was stunned. Had she agreed to this yesterday? What about her flight tomorrow? She could not think straight at all.

"But my flight, tomorrow I have to return home."

Miguel frowned. "You are home, right here in Mallorca. You know it's true. Yesterday we decided. I decided. I thought . . . Please tell me you haven't changed your mind, Maria."

Mary's confusion was etched on her face. So Miguel had proposed, but she had no recollection of accepting him. Had she?

Miguel seemed convinced that she had. "The sudden storm, everything happened so quickly. I wasn't sure," she said.

"And now? In the bright light of day? Be very sure. Tell me that you'll marry me, very soon."

"Yes," she replied, smiling happily. "Yes, Miguel, but I still have to go back to England first. I can't simply run away."

"Of course, I'm being selfish. We must phone your mother and break the news. We'll let your employers know that you've resigned. Next week we'll both fly to London so that I can meet your family, but today I'm taking you to my home, querida, O.K?"

"Whatever you say. It's as well you think for me just now. I'm not sure I'm able to think for myself at present."

"I'm being—what's the English word for the way I've taken over?"

"Bossy?" Mary said, smiling broadly. "I really don't mind."

When they arrived at the Gonzales villa at Lluc Alcari, Mary phoned her mother to tell her she would not be flying home the next day, and the reason why, so now they were both in shock!

She was then welcomed and shown to her room by the house keeper, a motherly soul who lived close by in a cottage on the estate.

"Hurry back," Miguel had said. "I'm afraid you may disappear if I let you out of my sight for long."

Mary unpacked quickly in her delightful room which opened onto a flower filled courtyard. She was still in a state of disbelief about the pace at which her life was changing. Was she just dreaming?

Bernado was in Palma so they lunched alone, on the broad verandah overlooking the olive terraces to the sea. Miguel told her that his brother approved of the marriage. "He's a romantic himself and he refrained from brotherly warnings against hasty marriages. He understands how it is to be in love."

That afternoon Miguel started a portrait of Mary. He was so impatient to have it finished that he used watercolour rather than oils. "There'll be plenty of time later for oils," he declared.

As instructed, Mary wore red and held a gardenia. She was surprised that she was able to sit still so long. It was only when Miguel laid aside his brushes, came over and kissed her lightly that she realised how stiff she was.

"I've let you sit too long, darling. I'm sorry," and his touch as he massaged her neck and shoulders was both soothing and erotic, and the painting was temporarily forgotten.

That evening Bernado welcomed her most warmly. "Miguel is a very lucky man," he said. "Welcome to our family." They drank to the future and discussed plans for the wedding.

By Thursday the painting was finished and flights had been booked for Sunday afternoon. Miguel was pleased; pleased with the painting and pleased that he had insisted on going to England with Mary. He wanted to meet her family, to be with her, to be sure she would not escape! It would also enable him to save Bernado a trip, as he would be able to visit the London agents.

"Before you leave for England Miguel, you must visit great aunt Conchita. Take Mary over to meet her. You're her favourite, you know," Bernado added without rancour.

"Yes, of course," Miguel replied. "We'll go tomorrow afternoon."

On their way to Valldemosa Mary broke their companionable silence rather abruptly: "Do you believe in reincarnation?"

Miguel was surprised by the suddenness of the question, but saw its significance at once. "I would like to believe it, yes. I should be happy to think that my soul, that our souls will return again to earth." And though each knew the other's thoughts, neither voiced them. They were content that they had found each other in the present.

"My aunt has some extremely English habits," Miguel said. "Afternoon tea is one of them. I know you will like each other. She's very old and almost blind now, but still very full of life, and a sensitive pianist."

As they drew up beside the broad verandah, they heard the lyrical sounds of a Chopin waltz. "You see, all my family are romantics! That's my aunt playing. She spends a great deal of time at her piano since her sight failed. By the way, she doesn't speak English so I'll have to interpret."

The piece of music came to an end and they entered the drawing room unannounced. Mary was immediately impressed by the serene beauty and presence of the lady who rose to greet them.

"Miguel nino, it pleases me that you come to visit." She extended her hands for Miguel to hold. He kissed his aunt and introduced Mary, whose hands were clasped by the elderly lady. Her touch was both welcoming and searching. She spoke a few words and Miguel said "My aunt welcomes you and says she is sure you will be happy here. She has always judged character by people's hands, and especially now, and your hands are good hands."

The strong sun bothered the old lady, so she ordered tea to be served indoors. While they waited, Miguel and his aunt conversed a little in Spanish and Mary looked around the cool, flower filled room. There was a sharp intake of breath as her eyes looked into those of a portrait on the wall facing her; it might have been a looking glass, for the face she saw was her own. Even the sitter's hand, as it held a gardenia, could have been her own hand.

Miguel heard the intake of breath and felt the tension. He looked first at Mary, then followed her gaze to the picture. He too was unnerved by what he saw, by what he must have seen a hundred times before, and he realised why Mary had seemed so familiar.

"Quien es ella?" he asked. "The woman in the portrait, who is she?"

"The one in the red dress? Little is known for sure, but I was told she was betrothed to my grandfather, your great grandfather, but she died before they were to marry. One story says she fell to her death from Cap Gros, but no-one really knows. My grandfather's signature is in the corner, so I suppose he painted the portrait. You inherited his talent as well as his name."

Miguel went to look at it more closely and as he touched the frame the cord broke, sending the picture crashing to the floor. The fragile backing splintered and when Miguel picked up the canvas he saw the inscription on the back: "Maria, siempre, Miguel".

He swallowed hard, deciding that Mary should not know the story he had just heard, at least, not until they were safely married and she had indeed come home.

A SONNET TO REASON

My home, my friends and those I loved the best,
All these I left, and quickly wondered why.
Each person whom I met asked: "Why invest
Your time abroad and like the swallow fly
To warmer lands as summer months decline?"
No answer could I give: I knew of none.
It should have stirred my motives to define
My reasons why. But then, I knew no one
The need of whom would make me alter course.
I sought I knew not what, to find too late
A soul like mine, a strong compelling force
Which cried out: "Stay, for I will compensate
For what you seek and have not known before."
Too late I knew, but time may chance restore.

THE GIFT

Luke sat at the piano, oblivious to the audience, completely lost in the music he was playing, creating would be a better description, for his hands coaxed an almost tangible shape from Beethoven's Moonlight Sonata.

Linda stood in the wings watching her talented son perform. She felt so proud of him and his great achievement. It was a gift, of course, this talent of Luke's, but one which seemed to contradict Linda's earliest expectations for him. Still only twelve, he could play any music by ear having heard it a couple of times. As she listened, his mother thought back over the boy's life and tears welled up as she remembered.

* * * *

Luke and Emma were born during Linda's second year of marriage to Bob and the twins' arrival completed their perfect family. Passers-by had frequently commented upon the beautiful babies when Linda had taken them to the park or shopping. Though both were fair like her, they had Bob's deep brown eyes, a compelling combination. Though they looked very much alike, Emma had a sunny, outgoing temperament, while Luke was solemn and unresponsive.

At bathtimes Bob helped if he were home in time. It was apparent early on that while Emma enjoyed the contact, laughing and playing as she was bathed and dried, Luke submitted to it without enjoyment, and seemed relieved when bathtime was over. In spite of Bob's efforts Luke remained aloof.

"He's just not frivolous like Emma," Linda observed. "He's going to be a great thinker." But she had her doubts.

As the months passed the contrast between Emma's liveliness and Luke's lack of response did not lessen. Linda sought reassurance from their G.P. He examined the children and declared both of them fully fit, attempting to dispel their mother's fears by saying that children develop at different rates and have individual personalities.

Linda remained unconvinced, her intuition telling her that all was not well. She remembered next a visit to the clinic when the twins were almost two. Both had been walking for many months and Emma wandered around the waiting room, her natural curiosity taking her to each mother and baby in turn.

"What a friendly little girl," another mother said to Linda. "She's a happy little soul."

Linda agreed that she always was.

"Isn't her brother feeling well then? He hasn't moved since you arrived," the woman continued.

"Oh, Luke isn't like Emma. I think he's going to be

a philosopher! He sits and thinks while Emma is never still," Linda explained.

Her neighbour spoke to Luke, smiling at him: "Your sister's making friends. Don't you want to make new friends?"

Luke turned away, his expression impassive. Linda took him on her lap, talking quietly to him but he didn't respond.

"Has he started to talk yet?" the woman asked. "Jamie never stops when we are at home. Much of it makes little sense except to him, but he never stops chattering. Your daughter seems the same."

Indeed she was. She was chattering fairly intelligibly to everyone in turn, having a high old time. Linda felt a chill, not for the first time, for Luke had yet to utter a single word, though he appeared to understand everything she said to him.

When her turn arrived, she expressed her concern to the sister in charge: "I'm sure he's not deaf."

The nurse took Luke, unresisting, upon her lap, but when she spoke to him he merely stared back, his eyes registering nothing. "Some children develop speech much later than others, Mrs Barrat, so there's probably nothing to worry about, but I'd like you to take Luke to see Mr Nash, a paediatrician at the County. I'll give you a letter to take."

Mr Nash gave Luke a number of tests beside a thorough physical examination. While he did respond to given instructions, his movements were mechanical and devoid of any interest whatever.

"It's too early to make a firm diagnosis, Mrs Barrat. I'd like Luke to see a colleague of mine, Mr Charters, for a second opinion."

"Tell me, Mr Nash, do you think Luke is brain

damaged?" It was the hardest question any mother could ask.

"No, Mrs Barrat, at least, not in the accepted sense."

Linda looked puzzled by his answer and asked him to explain.

"Luke's manipulative skills are excellent, and his co-ordination. Recognition is good too. He also understands the simple language we expect of such a young child. But he is very withdrawn. Do you talk to him, cuddle him?"

"I try to cuddle him but he seems to dislike the contact. He suffers it for a few minutes then wriggles free. I talk to both the children, all the time."

"Mmm. Is he active?"

"Not nearly as active as his sister. He appears to daydream."

"I'm sure there's nothing physically amiss — no hearing loss or damaged vocal chords — nothing to account for his lack of speech. I'll give you a letter for Mr Charters and I'll send him my findings. Don't worry Mrs Barrat, he's a very healthy boy."

Linda's stomach turned over when she read the plaque: "*F.E. Charters. Consultant Psychiatrist*". She had half expected it, yet it still disturbed her.

The psychiatrist gave Luke a great many tests. By the end of the consultation Linda was prepared for the worst.

"Mr Nash and I agree on a preliminary diagnosis, though with so young a child there's no absolute certainty. Have you heard of autism?"

"Yes," Linda replied in a small voice. "I've read an article about it at some time, but I really don't understand what it is."

"Well, we both think that Luke may be autistic. He

displays behavioural signs of the condition; but we are open to other possibilities at the moment."

"What causes autism?"

"No one is sure. I can recommend a book, but don't expect it to give you all the answers. It will help you to come to terms with Luke's apparent lack of affection. That doesn't mean he won't respond in his own way to your love and care. In fact I recommend that you treat him exactly as you treat Emma in showing your love, talking to him, cuddling him whenever you can, and so on."

"Will he learn to speak?"

"He may. It's quite likely he will, as most autistic people do in time learn to use language. Talk to him a lot, and never answer for him; be patient."

"How about schooling?"

"There are a few special schools, but not nearly enough. I'll give you a leaflet about them. You may wish to see some of them and put Luke's name on a waiting list," Mr Charters suggested.

* * * *

As the months passed, Emma's vocabulary increased rapidly but Luke still failed to talk. Emma seemed to know what her brother wanted without the use of words, which was uncanny but useful. Luke's greatest pleasure came from listening to music and he became unhappy and even slightly aggressive if his listening were interrupted. He sat close to the speaker, with a rapt expression on his face.

When Luke was four he had a toy piano, which he guarded jealously. This was a turning point for him.

Linda was preparing lunch when she heard the simple melody line of a Chopin waltz. Looking into the living room, she was amazed to see Luke's small fingers picking out the notes.

"Clever boy, Luke, that's very good," she encouraged him, and she thought she detected a smile.

"I couldn't believe my eyes, Bob," she told her husband that evening. "Play for daddy, Luke."

He played the same piece and Bob was astounded by the accuracy of the melody. At last there was something Luke really cared about and his interest was encouraged in every way.

For Luke's fifth birthday they bought him a second-hand piano which he played for hours at a time, showing an uncanny knack with natural harmonies. Having listened to a piece on the radio, he had no difficulty in reproducing it on his piano. He had found his personal form of communication. His parents were relieved and thankful for this blessing.

At six Luke was lucky to be accepted for one of the few vacancies at a special school for autistic children. There his phenomenal talent was encouraged and blossomed rapidly. He even learned to decipher the symbols on sheet music but preferred to play by ear. In time he became a little more sociable, joining in some of the activities with other children; but he was still preoccupied with music. Linda's and Bob's biggest disappointment was that Luke still failed to speak.

* * * *

As the last notes of Beethoven's Moonlight Sonata died away, enthusiastic applause filled the school hall, amidst calls of "Encore! Encore!"

Linda walked onto the stage and spoke to Luke, still seated at the piano.

"Everyone liked it, Luke. They want you to play the Minute Waltz. Will you play it for us?"

Luke looked up from the keyboard at his mother standing beside him.

"Yes Mother," he said seriously, his very first words, then he began to play.

EPITAPH FOR A POTTER

Earth, fire and water, basic as the air we breathe,
The potter takes to make his spirit yield.
Common clay and water, these he brings alive;
His mind's eye sees the form, his hands create,
Taming the wayward substance to his will.
His fingers, sensitive yet strong, must curb and train
    and mould.
He disciplines it, reins it in, with firmness, craft and
    care,
Adding a little of himself to every pot he makes.
Trial by fire next will prove the value of his work.
Sometimes an unseen flaw will crack or warp his
    ware,
But most survive the test and stand as tributes to his
    skill.
These he'll glaze and fire again with minerals the
    earth supplies:
Feldspar, dolomite and quartz, whiting, zinc and tin,
Rich browns from iron and ochre, copper green, and
    cobalt blue,
And manganese and nickel, vanadium and chrome.

And in two thousand years, if this mad world
    survives,
Fragments of his pots will be unearthed,

And knowledgeable men will nod and air their
    views,
Finding in the potter's work the facts they wish to
    see:
"Shards of a civilization spent", as men today will
    resurrect
Old Athens, Knossos, Rome and Tyre from bits of
    pots from long ago.
The potter then will smile, though he himself is clay.
He'll know that what they really see are fragments
    of his life:
His epitaph and obituary, written with water, fire
    and clay.

Martin, Lincolnshire 1978